# POST-URBAN SONGS

# POST-URBAN SONGS

## Collected Poems

## PATRICK GASPERINI

POST-URBAN SONGS
Collected Poems


Copyright © 2012, 2021 Patrick Gasperini





First published in 2012
Second edition 2021


ISBN 979-12-200-8464-2


Jacket design by Piers Tilbury

# ACKNOWLEDGEMENTS

Early versions of
*Untimely Dedication*, *Hymn to a Starry Birth*,
*A Midwinter Night's Dream*, *Into a Delphic Night*, and *Elegy*
were published as *Dionysian Poems* in
*Living Poets* Volume I Number VI in October 1995
by Dragonheart Press, Derby, UK.

Many thanks to Sean Woodward.


Extracts from other poems first appeared
in the following British magazines:
*Angel Exhaust*, *Fire*, *Rustic Rub*,
*Terrible Work*, *Tremblestone*.

Many thanks to the editors.


Extracts from some poems have also been published
in various *Locust Magazine* issues (ISSN 1529-0832),
online at https://www.locustmagazine.com.

To my mother Rita (1927–2015)
and my father Antonio (1933–2012),
who were proud of me.

# CONTENTS

# Untimely Dedication

To you, Aphrodite and all the silken condoms you have collected
    from all walks of life;
To you, polymorphous Priapus, protector of my illusions, right-
    wing swindler;
To you, whose tail can tear the veils of doubt,
Uncork all the cheapest bottles on the western sills, on the eastern
    shelves,
Collective hysteria;
To you, anorexic catfish, sophistic drag queens, Wall Street junkies;
To all of you, as well as to a crowd of others,
Unknown beyond stadium seats, cheerleading pimps and quacks;
To all those who sell clams and eels at street corners,
Their sperm a farthing a dram;
To drunken jesters by their chamberpots and fortune-tellers in
    their sleazy lairs,
Fear hunters, their ears and nails at ease, scaly spines and faces;
To all of you, and to all those who elucidate what I elucidate,
My poems I dedicate,
And I hope my name will burn in their hearts forever,
As their names and eyes and links will burn in my heart forever
    and ever.

# Early Fragments

# Stanzas

The wind, the peach, the green cicada
Are all my true companions,
As here I sit yellow and yelping,
Whimpering while I chop my last onion,
Waiting for daylight to wash my wrinkled scarf,
And bless my gangrenous leg despite a god's grudge.

Were I a king—why am I not a king
If one insidious way or another
We have all sped evolution?—
In return for a pinch of genuine waste,
I would give everyone an ounce of my bone marrow.

May my benevolence make you all happy,
And evoke socks you don't need to darn!
Upon my word—just lentils and happiness,
Love legends of my golden age.

*

Madly last night,
Wind-scorched, looked after by a clan of looters,
Sacred among whelks, whistles, and kegs of south-west warbles,
I was born once again.

Bankers and bakers left off work at four sharp,
A foundling was mistaken for a New Age fawn,
Teenage whores driven home in diamond cabs:
Let's go then, you and I,
It's market day beyond the bamboo village.

*

The twentieth leaf of my dishevelled years sprouted
When torchlight ravens nested in my hermitage,
And birthday geese honoured my nimble integrity;
No matter who kept watch at the secret back door,
I broke into the godfather's shop and stole his wisdom.

On the stroke of dawn,
A starfish engraved on her right ankle, crystal clogs,
Miss Josephine served hot lemon and sherry:

"A kiss, my lad,
The mystery of my syphilitic lyre!"

*

Who dares disturb Cassandra in her smoky cave,
Flint hips, biceps, green slime all over,
While for my wedding night, with ascetic skill,
She is honing her carving tongue?

*

Sitting by a Gothic candlestick, grey, absorbed,
A few pearls of arsenic,
Mr. Grace glanced at his chapped hands,
Before scrawling an insidious ideogram on a flyer:

MADAME FRACCI

IN

TCHAIKOVSKY'S SLEEPING BEAUTY
DOOMSDAY PERFORMANCE
TONIGHT . . .

A dragonfly could not ennoble his low-class bellows,
Nor could an aphorism bury his broken promise:
"Are you coming home late tonight?"

His wife, ready soon after tea,
Elastic, dense fluidity,
Responsive incongruity,
Stork legs, silk flags:

"Why don't you ever ask me if I am happy?"

# Postcards of a Psychedelic Holiday

O guardians in crimson cloaks, while the goblin service was being held beyond the lawn and an enormous glass gate. I only remember the lofty walls and the brown-eyed clock.

*

I dived into a wavy dream and set off for a green land on Saint Merlin's day. The clouds were grey bells, and the valley ran away in the morning wind. When I entered the ancient tower, I fell silent as if a meteor storm was about to break. I arrived at the peacock's house by noon, and a green-haired oak welcomed me. Later that afternoon, I visited the plain and the altar of the sun. The sky was as dark as a hangman's soul. A Gothic steeple and the white moon in the twilight.

*

Shakespeare's temple was as bright as a lamb's blood, whereas its wooden floor darker than the darkest corner of the cosmos. All of a sudden, the druids stepped out of the clouds. Their music! Their songs! That night I was told a supernatural tale because I was a Viking prince in the Triton's town. The realm of the flying cat!

*

Daybreak was grey and misty. When the horses' silver hooves hit the ground, smoke rose from it. A three-legged goddess gave the king a lightning spear . . .

*

I loved the wisdom of forgotten scrolls. One day I walked across a forest of priestly sounds and drums and flutes. I saw a hamlet beyond a labyrinth of branches and met the forest dwellers. I was the biblical knight who first discovered the serpent's beauty in a time-forsaken cavern. A crystal skull on a blue pillar.

*

Legions of warriors slept in their bronze tombs. Their flags were torn and blood-stained. Petrified monsters reigned in the underground castle, and I learned the stories of their lives as from a seer's globe. The city chanted the bizarre ballad of its birth.

*

I walked by without kissing Sleeping Beauty's cherry lips, and I sailed away on a cloudy afternoon.

## Morgause and Rebecca

MORGAUSE
> Only the country fiend who feeds on watercress
> And lunar dew can listen to the blue
> Hallucinations of our grubby brains,

Before profaning every cosmic law:
O secrets of your fingers, blessed knife!

REBECCA

Fear not, my friend. No horn, no liquid tail,
No sticky web; no crab will creep to you
To suck the vital nectar from your skull:
For you a Cyclopean bud tonight!

MORGAUSE

Take my indigent soul and set it free.

REBECCA

I will! Your blood is young, impatient, sinless,
And I will help you leave this hollow slum
And fly away, as if you were a swallow,
To reach a country where the sun is pink.

MORGAUSE

Hold my shaking hands and don't let them go:
Let's fly together to the fount of light . . .

# Hymn to a Starry Birth

## A Rhapsodic Poem

But not the stars; the stars came otherwise . . .
—Robert Browning, *Caliban upon Setebos*

# 1

I was told to listen for the sphinx-headed night was ready to speak,
The bonfire prelude was about to be announced to tabloid shacks
    and barbed-wire shrubs.

Tramps and pedlars came to my cradle, like the swamp, cable-
    bearded and mould-mottled,
Sleep-deep, they emerged around me,
Heavy with padlocks and safety pins, glinting and humming,
As if all their bells were berries in that boundless sky,
And blowlamp, like the swamp, and breathing earrings,
And one-eyed Shylock, brother of a clockwork spree.

The tramp patrol said, "It is you!"
The shantytown prince said, "It is you!" and no one else spoke;
Gunshot wounds bloomed on my back for six nights,
And on the seventh day their glory was offered in token of my
    love:
I evoke the angel that brought me to life,
I evoke and listen to her songs along rotting railings.

My mother told me to wait and I waited,
My mother told me to look and I looked.

Bless my days and nights, you long-eared playwrights, prowling
    around Venice cafés:
For my spirit shall have no end!

Bless my days and nights, you Lady Mojo pole-dancing in a Soho
    nightclub:
For my spirit shall have no end!

Bless my days and nights, you Miss Electra, black-and-white star-
    let walking up and down the Champs-Élysées:
For my spirit shall have no end!

## 2

A burglar crept into my toy coffer, and I heard my acid bottles
    weave a spell around him.

Urine-painted walls chimed brightly, and the two-faced ferryman
    sailed into the bipolar gorge,
Garret rats awoke to the cold sound of the horn up the stairway,
Heresy howled,
The rainbow dripped down like phlegm.

I saw the plague rise from the infected chisel,
I saw the bagpipe rain,
I saw plastic eggs hatched in a basement laboratory,
A fisherman camping on the steps of a poisoned latrine,
Tooth collectors, skull engravers.

Hallelujah for the almighty chainsaw, the throne where a stony-
    broke gigolo awaits the end of the night!
Hallelujah for the kettledrum dive, the fabulous well where the
    rapist quenches his fears and the needle sings!

I blessed myself crouching down in the guise of a grass-clad
    gambler,
The taxi driver's shotgun pealing in the foaming cloud inn,
A grog-forging god.

Good night now, smoking wreck at the bottom of the riot alley!

Good night, growling dogs at the foundry gates!
Good night, raving gutter, unknown heart in the flashing mid-
    night bus!
As the snow was falling dumb and heavy down Salcombe Hill's
    hairy back,
Into my triangle hands,
My heart's cogs.


# 3


I fell asleep as the first flamingo was being hanged in a freezing
    arcade,
And I dreamed of someone humming *O Sole Mio* on my tin skull:
It must have been windy that night, for I heard crane arms moan-
    ing in the distance.

"Follow me," said my Maternity Ward Quasimodo.

Lord of the ripe nipple and the ovarian warlock,
Lord of the butcher at work, of the hacksaw as well as of the ampu-
    tated foot,
Lord of the mulligatawny pot,
Of the drunken whore weeping at the bus stop every Saturday
    night.

Follow—he said—
The bottomless swamp and its claws of rot and bliss,
Behind a graffiti fence, sniffing the acid-smelling wind,
When Mr. Coleridge drowses off after gulping down a bottle of
    bourbon,
A needle in his arm, a spoon giving out a sleepy adagio on his cof-
    fee table.

January was sitting cross-legged by his Thai hookah,
February chewing tobacco with his ebony teeth:
"I'm afraid of the dark, mummy!"
And she kissed me until I went to sleep again.

**4**

There will be no other night like this night,
The sky through the bounty killer's body, his invincible cleaver,
    his wing-buckled boots.

The moon is a ghostly gamekeeper,
The moon is a smoky gambling alcove in Chinatown,
The moon is a blind Smith & Wesson in a hamlet feud.

The alchemist stops at the street market to sell his swamp tablets:
Those who yield shall be lost forever!

The alchemist takes off his fur cloak and the angel of death starts
    waiting on him:
Those who yield shall be lost forever!

The moon has starved forty centuries in the wisdom well,
The moon chants her psalms like a bawd in her boudoir,
The moon chains the one-eyed centaur to her torture couch,
The moon haunts the Sundown Hotel like a suicidal soul.

At the sign of the Hangman's Hood the publican fills his mug and
    drinks my health,
His daughter sits up late for me;
A rabid dog keeps me company on my way home, sulphuric stig-
    mata sizzling in my hands,

But can those dark paths give me anything more inebriating than
   what I can give back to them when I kneel down and kiss the
   one I cannot live without?

## 5

My friends are coming now,
I can hear them panting up the stairs, the floor planks squeaking,
Here they are!
Smell of chopped onion wafting through the window, mixing with
   their viper lips.

I idle away my Christmas Eve at the Parable Posada, a horned ser-
   aph sitting on my bottle,
I dance among smugglers and false prophets,
A gipsy girl initiates me into the ineffable tips of her tongue,
When I kiss her goodnight, she discloses all her leafy intrigues.

No one wants to absolve me, but I thank them for their useless
   sermons all the same,
Disdainful of religious etiquette, I make the most of the holy com-
   motion and run off with the rector's wife.

I approve of the sacred union of the human flesh and a sex doll,
Of the silk rope around Porphyria's neck,
Of Delphine kissing her naked reflection in a mirror,
And Hippolyte slashing her wrists at the Ritz Hotel.

## 6

Do you know where the mescaline wizard spends his long winter
   nights?

Do you know why Gobseck dug his safe in the redbrick wall?
Do you know where the bus-station whore takes her casual soul
    mate in the twilight?
Where the doorsteps reek of decaying urine?
Where you are what I am and what I am not?


For I can see your eyes when you hide in the undergrowth,
For there is the divinity of a deadly virus embedded in your long
    lashes.


I foretell that your body is holier than an outbreak of smallpox,
I foretell that your perversion on a park bench electrifies genera-
    tions of split personalities,
I foretell that nothing lives forever, but your evil lies live forever
    and ever.


For your second client mistakes your nipples for two gold molars,
For your flashing whip cleanses at once roots and leaves.


The mysticism of rum and tequila is yours, rosemary and arsenic,
Harpsichord at dawn, cymbals at dusk.


For your belly is a Jurassic valley and your navel Judas' chalice,
For the alley leading to the killing spinney leads to you,
For only the solitary pilgrim knows of the path to your crossroads
    garden.


I translate you into the underworld language, silken noose around
    my neck,
The clean machete shines like you, the machine gun flashes like
    you in the dark:
Hallelujah! Hallelujah!

## 7

Henceforth I will be driving a cart loaded with salt and second-
hand crosses;
Henceforth I will be bursting into the village church to scare all
the children away;
Henceforth, half-naked and proudly stoned, I will be haunting the
ladies' room at the Paris Opera House;
Henceforth handcuffs and tarragon, wreaths and leather straps,
Diving merlin into a petrol pond and then up to the stars with a
chopped finger in my beak,
Bags of rattling bones as trophies,
Mr. Jack Knife, morphine and hyssop!

Where your legs fork and Othello buried his wife's innocence,
I'll sneak out of your jeans and listen to the incredible excuses of
your torn knickers.

The gang leader shot twice, and I didn't stand aloof any longer;
The scouts came back after dark, their pockets bulging with wed-
ding garters,
The one who joined us on second thoughts was welcomed as our
blood brother at once.

I was invited to the smuggler's cabin on the Sea of Galilee;
He didn't believe in reincarnation or predestination,
But in salted sardines, Marlboro broth, and Caribbean rum:
"Dance for me, O Mary Magdalene: here's the pope's head on a
silver platter!"

When everyone got drunk, she snuggled down beside me,
Red pebbles, moth petals;

By sunrise we were out to sea again,
Charon on the lookout by the helmsman,
Impenetrable fog, voices whispering in the distance,
The weatherman had forecast rain by noon, but there was no rain
    until the close of the day.

A teenage junkie asked me to stay with her the rest of the night:
Hurray for both of us, indigent man and wife!
Monkeys on the mantelpiece, messengers from Cromwell Street,
Doll arms and legs in a coffer under our bed:
Hurray! Hurray!

# 8

Despite what my teachers used to say,
Yes, ladies and gentlemen, I know all the books by heart;
Now I uncork my last vintage bottle of moonshine,
I no longer fear to show my angle of wisdom where my crotch
    swells up,
Axioms and thunderbolts, radius and centre,
And from the remotest recess in my body I pick up a lilly and of-
    fer it to the first maths teacher wearing a thong.

"Wait," said my long-expected friend,
"For Cerberus at your feet, red-light district, sylphs in spicy
    brandy,
And on a Sunday evening, syphilitic priests barbecuing Mary's
    placenta,
Crimes in a primary school lavatory,
Because our deadly sins are nothing but marvels out of their
    prayer books,
Hunting tongues howling across the city dump,

Unholy relics, blood-stained aprons, chicken entrails,
Queen Spider and King Trefoil."

Good morning then, night-shift nurses in miniskirts!
Good night, Catfish Lane scum!

And everybody came, like the swamp, cable-bearded and mould-
    mottled, and the door was bolted behind them,
As the snow was falling dumb and heavy,
On the tyre ditch,
On our neighbour's car wreck.

That night my mother told me of sparks, logs, mistletoe, lanterns
    in the flashing dark,
And on that long night my father knelt down and kissed me for
    the first time.

# A Midwinter Night's Dream

## A Mock-Shakespearian Interlude

Hast thou entered into the treasures of the snow?
—Job 38:22

# 1
# (Hermia and Demetrius)

DEMETRIUS (*to himself*)

It is winter where streetlamps are unbreakable chains,
Where blurred staircases hide the mystery of dark love,
And topless fairies leave their fishnet lairs and wink at ghostly
cars:
This is the tale of acid hissing in our syringe, heaps of snow on
the fence,
Of love euphoria on a dirty park bench.

HERMIA (*to herself, entering*)

Who was the one snoozing under the fire escape in the moon-
shine draught when the party was over,
Chloroform-smelling, steel stitches on his forehead?

DEMETRIUS (*turning around*)

O Hermia, are you still daydreaming?
Then close your eyes again and dream about my hand slinking
into your sloping shrubs.
Do you remember the night we first met on the moon-rave
roof?
Two white pebbles in my handkerchief and your eyes as wet as
ashen grass?

HERMIA

Did a bristly snowstorm explode in our blood and brains soon
afterwards?

DEMETRIUS

Do you remember what happened then?

*(Hermia lowers her eyes. Demetrius touches her hand, but she steps
away.)*

Hermia

> Have you seen Lysander, Demetrius, his sleet-white lips and
>> eyes?
> No one has seen him since the loudspeakers caught alight and
>> off he darted.
> I last saw him in agony on a bench in the booze-up breeze,
>> howling in a donkey cloak . . .
> Have you seen him?
> I fear someone loves him so much as to shoot him in the head!

Demetrius

> O Hermia, if this will make you smile again,
> I'll jump off a bridge, a rope around my neck,
> Or I'll drink a hemlock cocktail to celebrate,
> But I cannot tell you what I have never seen or heard.

Hermia

> Shush! Someone's coming—is anyone coming?

Demetrius

> It might be Oberon and his garage gang, home after work,
> Boars in blood-soaked rags . . .

Hermia

> It's Lysander! I know it is him!

Demetrius

> Poor Hermia, your brain is a scrambled egg,
> But I can only afford a corrupt dose to cheer you up,

For I am just a penniless cripple now.
After cleaning out all my secret safes and drawers,
My whores ran away in the dead of night,
And I have to tell you this, my sweet:
By your dear Lysander they've all been hired and branded.

Hermia

O Lysander! My Lysander! Will you ever hug me again?

# 2
# (Demetrius and Bob Goodfellow)

Bob Goodfellow (*carrying a shoulder bag*)
Here I am from a land where streets smell of dry blood,
Where men are grey-capped snakes and women easy vestals,
Rabbit-fur hands, croaking slit throats, bullets sold in cereal
    boxes, cold-blooded,
As well as rapes lurking in the likeness of babysitters,
And Princess Snow I think waking up,
Giving thanks to the new-day shoot-out,
Snorting, sneezing,
Whirling, wailing,
Blah blah blue bleat—
In short, again here I am!

Demetrius
Night is falling,
And at nightfall I knew you were skulking through shrunken
    head bushes,
Leather coat, drag-queen boots,
And in that goatskin bag hanging from your shoulder,
Are you hiding a glass box?

BOB GOODFELLOW

> If you think I'm coming from a haunted forest around Athens
>> with a Christmas present for you,
> Dear Lord, you're higher than I thought.
> Although every night along Boulevard Saint Michel I offer vi-
>> brations to ladies in distress,
> My favours are not flatulent foibles in a youth-hostel room:
> How much would you pay for my pious service?

DEMETRIUS

> Everything, my angel of death!
> You can have my silver spoons and forks,
> My teddy-bear collection,
> Even Hermia à la carte, her tinsels and tassels,
> Twice, only tuppence from dusk till dawn.
> No mercy on the thief who stole the snow from my safe!
> What did King Baker feel when the flour for his birthday cake
>> was crawling with maggots?

BOB GOODFELLOW

> Your words are sweeter than the moon sinking into a stew pot,
> Or blood singing on my rusty-bladed knife,
> For generosity isn't my mortal virtue.
> It is time, therefore, to unwrap your long-expected gift—

DEMETRIUS

> Stop raving!
> Don't keep me waiting as though I were outside a gents door, a
>> whirlwind in my bowels.

BOB GOODFELLOW (*fishing a big flask out of his shoulder bag*)

> Here is Lysander's head in vinegar preserved!

# 3

# (Demetrius' Soliloquy)

DEMETRIUS (*to himself, sitting on a bench at a bus stop, holding a bottle of whisky*)

Thunder keeps on clapping in my head,

For tonight I've been flogged and crucified, O foulest plot!

Hermia will no longer come back to my chiming loft, across
     from Don Vito's wine shop, bobbling and slobbering.

O Don Vito, my underworld comforter,

Thank you for selling me your most mischievous demon.

Although I'm a tramp snoozing on a church doorsteps now,

Only talking to his corns, tinkling teeth in a piggy bank.

O! Look at my hands, sickly sweat,

They can only shrink and shake,

It is time for vengeance—fire in my stomach and a blizzard in
     my dreams.

Mosquito net gleaming like tears and whips in a witch's shack,

Shrouds melting away, Salvador's clocks,

Gabriel's sex appeal, spider's coup de grâce—his perfidy:

Maldito! Exécrable! Exécrable!

O Lord Macallan, help me find a wise razor to slit Bob Good-
     fellow's neck,

And a strong hook to hang my Hermia from, tied up upside
     down, a quartered cow,

To let her gently bleed to deserved death.

All in all, I have mistaken a cheap harlot for Joan of Arc,

And a toffee-snatcher for Sir Jimmy Tyrrell,

Low-class Arsène Lupin.

Nothing more to say.

Adieu!

     Burp, burp . . .

# Into a Delphic Night

## Picaresque Tableaux

# 1

One summer night, after my last pint of stout,
I took a bow and followed a circus caravan as it bumped away into
    the midnight razzmatazz,
When stories were told about a tavern where free grog was offered
    to Holy Land travellers,
When an oil lamp was burning on a crate of imported maize, the
    key forever in the lock.

Skull jugglers, firework eaters, tightrope nymphomaniacs, their
    long tails and razor fingernails,
An African queen's head on the mantelpiece, her ebony milk and
    snapdragon fangs,
All dissembled in cardboard coffers,
One-eyed salesmen who spend their nights in their convertibles,
Cheddar sandwiches and ginger ale, but worth a dinner at the
    Plaza,
Pink pot kegs, gateway to the Mermaid Tavern.

I asked for some more bouillabaisse and a goblet of Pinot Noir,
A Flemish merchant across from me lit a Montecristo,
His walking staff a water serpent, a skeletal nymph sleeping at his
    feet.

I asked the maître d'hôtel how old the chambermaid was,
A refugee from the Garden of Eden;
I followed her through corridors and empty rooms,
Her legs and breasts bellowing and grunting as she stripped off
    her veils and stepped into her bath.

She gave me everything although I didn't ask her for anything,

Glistening with home-made spirits, curtains flapping in the des-
   ert moon, fat ox heart;
Her hemlock breath was enough for me,
Her womb a brazen spittoon where I could drown my diffidence.

The lorry driver was never back home before daybreak,
His nineteen-year-old wife, a nimble wild goat, unlatched the back
   door and waited,
Her coconut breasts blurring in the candlelight,
And in the dead of night someone sneaked in like a weasel,
Two shadows wallowing together in the same bed in the dead of
   night.

The lorry driver every night at Uncle Pablo's Posada till daybreak,
His bottles and casual friends,
Their coarse hands, their reckless jokes, their mellow innocence.

## 2

There was a house across the street, a haunt of rogues and sailors;
Twelve girls and none of them over twenty-five,
Twelve girls the old lady loved, her own daughters though they
   were not:
The crow-haired girls from Salonika, the mare-legged girls from
   Andalusia and Castile.

The old lady always behind their doors, always in their rooms,
The old lady, sixty-nine and always so eager to cuddle her twelve
   daughters' bodies.

Along the corridors she walked close to them, and one by one she
   undressed them,

And with each of them she felt the cool water down her back,
　　crawling on her buttocks,
And in the same bed she lay beside each of them and their un-
　　known guests;
It was the old lady who made them wriggle and quiver and moan.


3


The White Queen and the Black Queen sleeping hand in hand on
　　the same couch,
Hand in hand gliding away in the moonlight,
Running into a turquoise creek, two spirits splashing each other
　　merrily.


The White Queen's sun-smelling body as well as the Black
　　Queen's,
The White Queen lingering on the Black Queen's neck, on her
　　hazel nipples,
Their souls melted together.


I don't know why I accepted her invitation:
I knew none of her guests, nor did I know the fox-lipped hostess
　　sitting on her Venetian settee,
A string of musical pearls around her neck,
A Belle Époque cigarette holder, a butterfly crucified on her right
　　thigh,
My head in a dustpan, clean-shaven and -cut, a collectable item,
O breasts like bronze globes!
O biblical tension of her buttocks!


The monkey-woman struts around with no panties on,
The python-woman whips out her long tongue shamelessly,

The mink-woman offers me a cup of poisoned champagne,
The owl-woman carves seven circles on my chest,
The raven-woman hammers seven stakes into my back,
The jackal-woman feeds on my rotting heart,
The leopard-woman, the kestrel-woman,
The vulture-woman . . .

How many sleeping pills are you going to take with your good-
    night whisky?

# Une Mauvaise Chanson

## An Atypical Epithalamium

# 1
# (Groom)

Insane inventor, I'll create a brave new world of my own,
Where beer and wine are free in shops and pubs around the clock,
Where squirrels hop and pee here and there while we are having
    our Sunday picnics in Green Park,
Where religious frenzy is the worst sin,
Where Plato comes back to life and raves at Hyde Park Corner,
Where *Snow White and the Seven Dwarfs* is the tale of a prostitute
    and a bunch of pimps,
Where Moll Flanders is a Red Cross nurse and Nancy a mission-
    ary nun,
And Freud and Jung run a tattoo parlour in Whitechapel,
And the Tower of Babel is no longer an evil metaphor but an ex-
    clusive hotel on the Caribbean Sea,
Where you and I, my dear, are going on honeymoon on Pluto,
Because we are getting married tomorrow.

# 2

# (Groom and Bride)

I ran away from home when I was seventeen, never to go back,
After stealing as much as I could from my father's wallet,
After beheading all my sister's dolls in revenge,
For none of them resembled you, O wild Bride! Extreme dream!
Because she had given away my first *Playboy* mystical session.

I have known you, my poison, since the day I was born, O cruel
    Bridegroom!
You were not the one who would sneak into my bedroom at night,

"Let's play!" he would say;
But I, a ten-year-old girl, just wanted to sleep and dream;
"I don't like this doll, sir."
"Your mum said you'd like it. Come on, I've paid her $100!"

Come and don't be late, my dear,
Night has fallen, but I am still awake,
Your glinting safety pins and hooks,
But no one will hear your footsteps on the frozen pavement:
Bring me a black cloak and some blood-red roses, and I will wel-
    come you home,
Because tonight is the last night,
Because we are getting married tomorrow.

# 3

# (Groom and Bride)

Today I am meeting my Bride,
Today I am meeting my Bridegroom.

My Bride is nothing like you would expect,
My Bridegroom is nothing like you would expect either.

My Bride is a call girl on the French Riviera, €1,000 a night;
My Bridegroom bones poultry in a slaughterhouse in Marseilles,
    €10,000 a year.

My Bride believes in Nostradamus' follies, O my Tarot Priestess!
My Bridegroom loves stalking freckled girls in school uniforms, O
    my sweet Maldoror!

My Bride has been smoking pot all night,

And she is going to vomit on the church steps;
My Bridegroom has drunk ten bottles of tainted wine,
And he is going to vomit right on the altar.

What surprises me most about my Bride is her silicone clitoris;
What surprises me most about my Bridegroom is his collection of
    obscene holograms.

O dear Bride, my little rabid mink, put on your Red-Death mask
    and all your leather straps!
O dear Bridegroom, my sky-eyed viper, grind your razors and
    scissors!
Because today is the day,
Because at last we are getting married today.

# Elegy

To a young woman
who died in giving birth to triplets,
one of whom passed away shortly afterwards.

*Elegy*

## 1

It was night, but no one slept,
For she who lay on her marble bed was not asleep,
But shrouded in a veil of silence and ice.

The wind stopped howling and the rain froze into leaden pools,
Bat-eared fog swelling street corners and underground stations,
A tramp took refuge in a dark alley and began to weep.

## 2

Ruthless January, boar-snouted robber, sharp-taloned hangman:
Which is your coldest day? Which is your coldest night?

January, there is ash but no fire in the black stove:
Which is your coldest day? Which is your coldest night?

January, there is a sleeping angel on the ebony altar:
Which is your coldest day? Which is your coldest night?

January, no wine will ever make me happy again:
Which is your coldest day? Which is your coldest night?

O January, let me kiss her and fall asleep in her silvery arms again:
Which is your coldest day? Which is your coldest night?

## 3

We picked three young roses,
The colour of her eyes, the colour of a May night,
Their scent was the scent of her silken lashes,

And those three roses we loved, wrapped in a crystal veil, we
    offered to her.

We thought of her that day,
And the day before that day and the day after that day,
When we were sitting among a crowd of unknown people, waiting
    for the Bride to come,
But it was not the White Bride we were waiting for, but the Black
    Bride crowned with purple carnations.

As she passed by, a hand kissed her and dozens of other hands
    kissed her,
Friendly hands in love with her, though unknown to her,
But she could not feel their vital warmth,
Nor could she smell the scent of our young roses.

# 4

You must no longer weep, for she is now beside you;
You were told not to weep for she would return.

As soon as you wake up, you will realize that she is already there,
Immaterial, but still brimful of love, still in love with you,
Her consoling hand already on your cheek;
When the key turns in the lock, you can hear her heart throbbing
    behind the door,
But she hides away at once and you cannot see her,
Yet you can feel her holding you by the hand wherever you go.

When one day your children ask you where their mother is,
You will not show them the stone prison where she lies,
But, looking at the impenetrable night sky, you will say,

"She is the star that wakes you up in the morning, touching you
    with its diamond wings."

## 5

We can see the young mother, the immensity of her chervil heart,
On the starlit threshold, alone but smiling,
Waiting but never worried, waiting for her small child to return
    home and hug her again.

The young mother knows when her small child will return,
She is happy, for she knows where he is.

We know both the young mother and her small child,
We know that she will never forsake him, nor will the child for-
    sake her,
They will never forsake us.

## 6

Night after night and tear after tear,
We have finally seen through time's game and fear it no longer;
Though sad, we are no longer hopeless.

Bygone happiness and bygone sadness will never return,
Nor will the seasons when you were leafy and linnet ever return,
Nor will the day we called your name and you did not answer;
But although nothing ever returns, everything will finally meet,
For we steadily approach you as we move away from you,
And although now we are unable to fathom the adjacent image of
    things,
We'll soon know what you already know.

# A Metaphysical Mutation

## A Poetic Journal

"O Curtia!" said the hotel witch,
While contemplating the largo of a painted lake,
As if it were a window where stammering prayers had just been
    blown away,
Levels, garlic, useless graces.

You have not eaten anything for weeks,
Can a gem of rum give you back a spark of divinity?

It was raining, tropical meteors, perhaps bats,
Horses in the stable chewing gleams, cobwebs, and splinters,
Swinging signboard, as drunk as a ravenous orchid in the drizzle,
And shelves all around, home-made preserves and cheap tequila,
Velvety fumes of spirit and flesh,
In a tattered shroud, a trailer transformed into a shapeless mon-
    ster of rust.

You said you would never return, my child,
But I have been waiting for you ever since,
In my languid wound,
Essence of my memory.

*

You arrived in a downpour of green needles.

How beautiful you were, Curtia,
Gothic, lucent, muscular, a freshly whetted dagger,
Your hair a black octopus.

I wanted to tell you that you were a labyrinth of lines and asyn-
    chronous rings,
Aromatic light, sound from a spiritual fountain,

Material sighs and immaterial snares,
Symbolic helium,
Premonition.

"O happy couple!
Just married like two swans, I suppose?"

The bridegroom an exotic god;
His rapacious irreverence inebriating the ceremony,
Garland waistcoat and ermine dinner jacket,
His roaring voice a tomahawk in the back.

"You're going to be the happiest couple in this unhappy universe!"
Said the priest, kissing the fern-legged bride on the lips.

Room 13!
The key became a heron in your hand,
As you walked upstairs beside your husband, sometimes holding
    him by the hand,
The ivory muscles of your legs, the saffron skin of your legs,
Ragged assonance, poisonous balance.

Good night, impotent rodents!
I am going to show you my brave heresy.

(The bridegroom reminded me of my ascetic husband;
He wished to be buried under the signpost where the burning
    bush had first talked to him.

Impure champagne turned his walk home from the Folies Bergère
    into a trip to Damascus,
His donkey ears into Saint Paul's wings,

A fornicator into a new apostle in the shade of a feathery halo.

That very night he told me he worshipped the Indian Ocean,
Coral, scallops, and cuttlefish,
And we would all become seaweed sooner or later.

When the police stormed in one rainy morning,
I thought they would tell me he had flown away with a seraphic
    horde,
But instead of prayer books they found forty crates of Cuban to-
    bacco in our storeroom.

I spent that night in jail and seven more nights, but my husband
    did not turn up;
He turned up neither the next autumn nor the next winter,
Nor ever again . . .)

While you were walking upstairs beside your husband, sometimes
    holding him by the hand,
O my Curtia, the key a branding iron,
What did you think would become of you?

*

My house was but a worm-eaten castle on a crocodile river:
My father would tell me that crocodiles ate anything whenever
    they didn't have enough virgins for breakfast—even tricycle
    tyres.

This is the market square where slaves were auctioned every Fri-
    day morning,
Titans coming from the bowels of Mount Tambora,
Ebony goddesses, oceanic,

Who could break chains no elephants had ever broken,
Who could cause primeval floods whenever they urinated,
Octagonal anthills instead of breasts,
Clanging bell towers instead of toes and calves.


A young girl was delivered of her child under that cherry tree over
    there,
A stillborn child;
She did not mourn, though:
She knew her child would soon belong in a starry spiral.


O my father!
He loved the grocer's teenage daughter,
Her gazelle legs,
Her rosebud breasts,
Her swan-lake eyes:
That is why he never came back when he went out fishing for
    salmon one summer evening.


Whose body was that—headless, half eaten by crabs and sirens—
    that a tramp found on the edge of a rainbow swamp eight
    months later?


My brother thought he would become a celestial emperor
If he managed to pee in a crocodile's throat unharmed;
I don't remember him ever doing that,
But I remember him peeing in our mother's marjoram pots one
    April afternoon.


He told me he had seen a mine troll assault our mother in the
    woodshed,
He saw them struggle in the straw, hissing like rattlesnakes;

Although I was six, I didn't believe him:
I already knew mine trolls did not exist.

A goddess must be like you, Curtia,
Dark and impenetrable, as flexible as a cruel cane.

Your shadow a nebula on our bedroom rugs,
Your hair poison ivy,
Your eyes jaguars,
Your breasts anvils,
Your lips razors,
Your legs biblical pylons!

At seventeen, my brother was a Yellow Sea pirate.

Someone said that the nameless woman seen naked and merry in
    a moonlit field a few days before the spring festival was our
    neighbour's wife, a thirty-year-old nurse of Italian stock,
    whose buttocks my brother compared to Corinthian capitals.

Two days later, our neighbour's wife, my brother, and his orange
    van were gone.

I saw our neighbour sitting stock-still on the doorsteps week in
    week out,
Swearing loudly every now and then,
A bottle of mountain dew beside him, a revolver in his pocket.

When autumn came, he disappeared like pink mist,
Or was it just a heap of weightless dust that the morning wind
    blew away?

*

I only earn a few quid a month, but I am happy among shelves and
    spiders,
Mr. Longanotte ever so proud of me,
As I fly around in my frock of sea flowers.

Mr. Longanotte, a glossy watermelon,
His bow tie a red louse on the white continent of his shirt,
His trousers swallowing the whole Amazon jungle.

His nose a barbed-wire coop,
His neck an oak stump crawling with psoriasis;
He wrote a song for me about a sailor and his concubine:
"A drop I'd like to taste, just a drop from your flowery well, and I'll
    give you a rise overnight!
Is one quarter of your salary enough?"

And since that summer afternoon, when bunches of locusts were
    hanging from trees like bananas,
A plastic jellyfish, unable to speak or think,
That's what Mr. Longanotte is now.

*

My husband is a warehouse bard,
Boxes of Mediterranean oranges, lime, Malaysian tea;
After a ten-hour shift, at supper time,
He only talks of flying invoices and teddy-bear rats.

"Turn on the radio!
Glory to the Devil and his short-wave burps!

"Have you heard of the story of the skull hidden in a shopping bag?

The soft skull of a roadhouse waitress, fed up with her husband
    and underpaid job, who ran off with a Persian prince, a lugu-
    brious biker who ordered a taco one blood-shot evening and
    fell for her?
He took her away in his flaming chariot and promised he would
    love her more than a free provision of petrol;
But he was neither Persian nor a prince,
After offering her a rat-poison fag, he chopped her up into tiny
    stars of flesh."

I did not want to be like my mother:
Her bed crawling with scorpions,
A yellow-eyed pirate who raped her twice a week.

Besides,

Dirty sheets
Sweat-stained shirts
Swollen hands and feet
Rachitic eggs
Scabby bread
Smell of gin and phlegm
Scarlet spittle
Drops of mud . . .

The first man was certainly made from a handful of camel's excre-
    ment,
Eve from a hazel branch.

I wanted to be a queen:
Queen of the lightning hill, innocent equators, methods, brainsick
    planets,

Queen of the ethereal boat that drops anchor in a tropical crypt,
Queen of metaphysical intrusions.

But where is my god of leaves and clouds?
His eyes at midnight?
His hair that can snare dreams in a musical web?
His hands that can halt the orbit of time?

"What the hell do you want a child for?
A porous head smelling of stale milk,
Teeth swimming like eels in greenish dribble . . .

"Do you know how much a damned sack of tea weighs?
And those rats, fatter than hogs, eager to snap at the treasure of
    your trousers if you snooze near one of their holes?

"I'll buy you a straw-headed doll instead."

*

It was summer again, another curfew summer,
The earth a frying-pan where humankind was being fried like
    onion rings,
And the rain—whenever it rained before sunset—malignant oil.

(No one was brave enough to venture out by day;
After dark, only bats as big as beavers.)

At two o'clock I opened the window to see if the rain had stopped;
It had been raining for seven days on end,
There were frogs and water voles everywhere;
Jacques was not home yet,
His hornet breath still a haunting presence.

My bed adrift in a breathing shell where I could expand like fog,
Fantasies piercing me, a jelly corpse,
Orgasms fertilizing the fields of Mount Olympus.

When you return home, covered with hairy moonshine,
Your pockets proud of their abnormal masculinity,
Your breath reminiscent of guttural cockroaches,
Ready to stuff your stomach with buttered self-esteem,
Ready to send forth idolatrous branches,
Ready to decompose,
Evanescent,
Viscous,
Gaseous,

I will be flying away like redemption.

"What was his name?" the hotel witch asked.

The name of a thousand angels.

*

There is a party at the Whispering Tower, are you coming?
You'll meet a crew of prophetic souls,
Druids of fluid dimensions.

My friends, amphitheatres, cylindrical shrines,
They float naked, absorbing seams and discrepancies,
Speaking the language of Arctic prairies, dancing like cheetahs,
Sea savannahs,
Hectic villages.

When the first trumpet was blown . . .

Perched on a canned beer peak,
A mermaid inviting me to drink up her frustration,
Oozing from her nipples as from a leak in a maimed pipe.

When the second trumpet was blown . . .

Armed with Caribbean drums,
Dead-end deities emerging from the alley foam to soothe our
     painful navels,
A new god assembling a new galaxy.

When the third trumpet was blown . . .

Tunes from whisky bottles telling me to proclaim the resurrection
     of daylight.

It is time to fell the tree of wisdom and make firewood;
Let us feed our ovens on philosophers' vertebrae,
And pound the nefarious words of preachers in our chamberpots;
Aren't astronomers' thoughts soft enough for tramps to sleep on?

Let us turn our memories into something quite different:
Oxygen, lymph, phosphoric moon,
Revolutions,
But is the cathedral of ages holy enough to sustain our meta-
     morphic creed?

Look! You too are turning into a new universe,
Far more ethereal than our split philosophy.

Be
Flamingo

Fire-tailed crane
Sparrowhawk
Swift!

It is time for you to sharpen your free will,
Castrate the colossal stupidity of continents,
Crawl into the orifice of the sky, where our sins are nothing but
    mellow wine.

Go now!
Into the moonshine jingle, raving barrels, growling slops,
Pyramids of tins and blisters, silver squeals,
Rags, croaking taps, gospels, glorified jackknives,
Poetic profanation.

Parasitic jungle of chains,
Cyanide jungle,
Smallpox jungle,
Aluminium syringe,
Helix,
Opal,
Lute.

*

The riot broke out on a Saturday afternoon,
Some loafers at a street corner were discussing what had happened
    the night before:
A boy of fifteen and a girl of fourteen, both from the ghetto, were
    caught stealing a van,
The boy managed to flee, the girl was brought in;
The police were rumoured to have raped the girl to make her give
    away her partner's name;

SWALLOW DIVE OF DEATH IN ATTEMPT TO BREAK JAIL, newspapers re-
   ported the next day,
The boy was eventually found in a slum ditch, five bullets in his
   belly.

The loafers were talking and drinking,
A police car drew up across the street, "Snakes!" someone yelled,
Two sturdy coppers jumped out, arrogant and voracious,
A baton suddenly struck here and there,
A flick-knife clicked open, a revolver cracked twice,
Someone fell.

All the ghetto gangs spotted their chance of glory and loot,
The Skulls, the Rippers, the Night Rats and many others,
They all swore to crucify the Mayor and his bureaucratic herd;
By midnight the streets were alive with petrol-bomb comets,
By one o'clock most of the town around the ghetto was on fire.

The fighting went on until sunrise,
From my den among the chimneys I saw every stone hurled, every
   bullet shot,
I was the leader of a rebellious multitude.

Three cinemas and a nursery school were set ablaze, ten buses and
   fifty cars destroyed—five police cars included—dozens of
   shops and a church plundered, the priest flogged in his vestry,
   millions of windows smashed . . .
At two o'clock a filling station blew up like a contaminated atoll:
Satan was back!

When the sun rose, the world fell silent,
I only counted the stars on the pustulous pavement.

*A Metaphysical Mutation*

*

I remember waking up when it was still pitch-dark,
Am I Clytemnestra, Copernicus, or Captain Long-Tail?

I remember seeing my taurine reflection float somewhere,
My clothes on an armchair were shells on a dead beach,
I tried to sew a cloak of smoke and dew.

When I opened the window, it was morning again.

I went out bereft of moral impetuosity, as white as a razor blade,
Amid a crowd of secretaries and shop-assistants,
Lilies, synthetic silk, forever on time,
A ladder on the ankle.

When I returned home after the rains, Jacques was still waiting for
    me, sitting in his favourite chair,
Still watching the telly, which had gone off heaven knows how
    many years before,
A monolith of slime and filaments,
Speechless, aubergine-bellied, vacuum-ridden—
Were there any traces of curare in his cider?

I sneezed and everything vanished.

It was not too late when I recalled your genital flamboyance and
    started back at last,
Was it?

# Hoberon[1]

How long within this wood intend you stay?
—William Shakespeare, *A Midsummer Night's Dream*

---

1. *Hoberon* and *Tytania* are not misprints but the real names of these pseudo-Shakespearean street dwellers.

# 1

I analysed the plan from the four cardinal points and made up my
    mind at last:
I was certain that something was missing in the biological curve,
Unless I built an intermediate pillar,
The domes of existence would fall in sooner or later.

I left the cage of stagnant egos where I had been confined
(I am still convinced that I was right:
Nothing but my pride can shape the veil of dimensions!)
And visited towns of visions and space, syllables no one had ever
    bisected before,
Because they had not been created yet—
Perhaps . . .

I had a sack with me, fisherman's silk,
An enormous funnel that I filled with all I needed,
On the eighth day of my eternity.

I searched every eddy and gaseous angle,
I found all the ingredients to cook my creative soup:

Musical iron,
Unwholesome semiquavers,
Fluid infrared principles,
Rainbow cables,
Plutonium skies,
Circumlocutions,
Obliquities,
Persistence
            and fusion!

Now
Chaos must become
Ribs, pelvis, glands, syrup, membranes, cerebral gargles,

To synchronize our syllogisms,
To proportion the globules to the radius,
To decode the metabolism of races,
Metamorphosis of metals and melodies.

Nothing is easier than forging a pious brain,
God's geographical tissue,
In the revolving bucket of human naivety,
Between planes of revelations.

My Creation!
Invulnerable as a corpse on a morgue table,
Brighter than an electric bayonet,
His abdomen a growling tangle of strings,
Cogwheels thundering in his elbows,
Grotesque amoebae adorning his ears.

Your throne in the zodiac of our souls:

Henceforth

You shall have dominion over the lymph of the universe!

## 2

Glorious night!
Time to put on a coat of viscosity and selfishness,
Is there any difference between the rain and the electric chair?

Why is *aftersupperatachinesebistro* always so deflecting and drilling?

O! O! O!
The wind is still blowing bubbles of chemical beauties into

Rag dolls'
Impervious
Holes
But . . .

. . . are they nymphs or flesh-eating vestals?
Repercussion of animal thunderclaps,
Harps, banjos, spinets, saxophones,
Here someone sells old musical rubbish, pinched from a monas-
 tery in Nepal,
Old Mr. Redstowitch with his four-figure grin.

Quid! Quid! Quid!
£1,000,000
Oceans!
Vortices!
Galaxies!
£!

Gold in a milk jug implores us for veneration:
If my fingernails smelled of cosmic dust,
My intestines—doctors say—would jingle with gold.

If my bladder were a spring cloud,
I would flood the Vatican Gardens;
The pope would be forever grateful to me,
I would have a front-row seat at the celestial matinée.

Aristotle was right:
A basket of inspired quavers contains both hell and heaven,
And God can be boiled down to a spoonful of musical porridge,
Infusion of credulous chitchat.

Here I am! One, two, three!
Sophisticated slaves, my sisters,
Rainwater perversion and gutter incantation,
Tonight I wish to drink kerosene and worship a Syrian Valkyrie:
There is still a cycle left, a pinch of strychnine in my pouch,
*Twinkle, twinkle, lousy scar*

etc.

Bizarre words I've never managed to learn by heart . . .

Will you wait for me,
My Queen?

# 3

Do you wish to hear a love song, my Tytania?
It's a pity you are only used to such treacle as

My love holds you by the hand and tells you that nothing is worth
    praising on earth but your eyes, and nothing is more valuable
    than your voice and the colours of your words.

I am a contaminated god,
A perverse aphorism,
And my verses smell of twisted marrow,
Spheres of virulent shame,
Insolent scum of wisdom.

My Tytania!
I love the way you conceal your platonic vices in a crevice,
The flaming slime you pass off as ambrosia,
Infernal medicine:
How much a bottle?


I love the liquid oxide of your heels,
The humming craters of your chin,
The way you pluck a swan for supper and play a rhapsody on its
    neck,
The way you take off your clothes as if you were peeling an onion,
And curse the woodworm tribes on your bedpost.


Taverns, shacks, rotten planks and apples,
You must all know
                  that
                      my Tytania,
My x-legged angel, my coconut sorceress,
Mountain of copper muscles and logs in tin stockings,
Labial Argonaut,
                  Stole the treasure of my biscuit box,
When out I strolled to light a cigarette.


O damned herbaceous kiss!


Your feet giving off cube roots,
Seismic waves crisscrossing your back,
Magnetic ulcers on your shoulders,
Your scalp crumbling like sand,
The syncopation of your dusty tresses—

Enough!

Before I go on playing my harp,
For love can neither make my wallet sing nor fill my trousers with
    gold nuggets,
Let me be frank with you, Fräulein,
My considerable sigh:
Give me my money back!


# 4


Empyrean reception at the Sultan's palace,
Banana tycoons, Californian gods, big bugs, sharks all invited
*R.S.V.P.*


I put on my Sunday best,
Top hat, white scarf and gloves, an Incan medallion I purchased at
    a jumble sale,
Hired a winged broom,
And went as happy as an embalmed elk.


"Good evening, Milord," said the Captain of the Guards,
Although I had not eaten for six days and my socks were *Vanity
    Fair* pages.


I was afraid someone might see through my mask of colours,
I hid under a table and waited;
A waitress flew by, but I had enough time to inspect her floral
    ankles and calves,
I knew she would soon burst into a curaçao bush.


The Sultan's daughter rode a tiger around the fountain,
Her hair could satisfy my thirst for plenitude,
The riddles of her shadows.

A flourish of trumpets announced the beginning of the banquet,
And I sat beside the Prime Minister,
Plato was not as wise as he was:
His precepts were greeted with handclaps and hallelujah.


"Social injustice—

        Divine!

Let the rabble believe we love them;
But how can we love their fish-glue bones?
Their potato-peel hopes?
Their breath reeking of failure?
We must teach them to work two centuries a day,
For toil purifies their souls, while money corrupts their incurable
    innocence:
Hasn't the prophet taught us that we can live on locusts and wild
    honey?
Equality is but a wizened turnip.


"Taxes—

       The keynote!

Let's tax their anaemia, the inflammable mix they breathe, their
    wrinkles, their cannibal bread, the holes in their shoes, their
    prayers . . ."


I agree! I agree!


We must make the most of their hollow bellies,
Use their blood as fuel for our financial factory,
Their tribulations as toothpaste.


"Do you think 15°C is the ideal temperature to serve a bottle of
    Château Lafite Rothschild?"

## 5

There is a merry house on the hilltop,
What can we find there?
There is a merry house on the hilltop.

Who lives in the merry house on the hilltop?
Who lives there?

If you want to run after the sun, my children,
Gaily and thoughtlessly,
And have your pockets forever full of his legendary coins,

Keep away from Mrs. Montiero's!

She had many lovers in her youth, but none of them an eclectic
    soul:
A salesman, a concierge, a glazier, a chemist, a stockbroker, a pri-
    mary school teacher;
Is there anything better than a bedroom chirping with seminal
    syrup to study human nature?

Do you know where my friends are?

*Sunseeds will never pester,*
*Razors will never fester,*
*Nor will milk ever blister,*
*In the wild-flood pink,*
*In the moon-tide sink*
*In the night-brain kink . . .*

When did you see them last?

Warlock beneath diamonds,
Jack Rabbit whooshing, whooping,
Earthquake Joe,
Full Stop?

If I down another keg, do you think my feet will turn into geese
    and my bottom into a tropical garden?
Will my friends return like buccaneers to their native island?
My guardian angel never listens to me, he's too busy swimming in
    his pool of whisky,
But I can still smell the metaphors of his decaying teeth.

What about her nebulous armpits?

A treasure of elastic ribs and cheekbones is buried in Mrs. Mon-
    tiero's cellar,
For Satan is said to have sown the universe with cracked skulls,
But we have only found bottles of vintage port.

Enough!

Have I ever told you that my wife eloped with her chiropodist?
I often wonder if we have the right to reproduce,
Anyway,
        Good night!

What if the hill retches like a tomb on doomsday?

## 6

When I came back after work, my wife told me it was my birthday,
Even though she could not say how old I was;

For this once she had cooked a dream-stuffed duck instead of bat
    wings,
The usual remedy for my latent impotence,
Stewed with thyme and butter, three times a week.

She had promised the fusion of brass,
Circumnavigation of taboos,
Rowdy fauns.

Hold it, my dear!

Before you start telling me how difficult it was for you to pick out
    hundreds of suitable jewels to stuff this august duck with,
Sit down and listen:

The crane was lifting a globe of leaden variations,
When the chain snapped,
The foreman and a young workman would have been served for
    Beelzebub's brunch,
Had they not changed into a couple of titmice.

Wasn't that a sign?

7

Before kissing you goodnight for good,
I want to tell you what my friend Rabenwald and I heard late one
    autumn night,
As we sat in the fireplace blessings,
After drinking all the wine the gods offered us,
Tavern at the foot of Mount Parnassus.

Some more mead!
           Ten gallons!
                      Our mugs are empty!
Can it raise a hanged hypocrite from the dead?
Fit for heretics and call girls,
Under the auspices of a scorpion's prayer on your plate,
Alcoholic ecstasy,
Worth a faithful wife—or is it a faithful wife that is worth an old
    hogsheads?

Let's pick up our sickles and forks,
Armed with shuttle and thimble,
My tongue a perfect lancet,
Braver than bacteria,
Romantic asthma,
The rack may be our reward—
More honourable than £10 a week!

Here is my army:
Carpenters, weather prophets, bricklayers, penniless veterans,
    stray cats, backstreet mentors,
Rhyming squads, hungry beasts, lonely death,
Our magic awareness,
Water, fungous cord, fat, fried factions and nothing else:
*Well done!*
        *Well done!*

We can no longer wait!
We have not polished our ploughshares in vain,
We have not gilded our ropes in vain,
We have gobbled rhapsodic hunger,
Our neurosis, cowardice, submission,

Flagons of worthless echoes,
Our ancestral indignation:

*Well done!*


We diffuse and dissipate,
We harmonize prophecy and smoke,
Abdomen and microwaves,
And dissect the idylls of oscillating oil,
Incompetent seams,
Organic scarecrows:

*Well done!*


Prostration and cholera cannot wait,
Our worn-out trousers,
Our cavern-bowels,
Our dynamos,
Our screws and nuts,
Our cymbals,
Translucence cannot wait:


Are we ready to sell off the glorious sun to the sleeping world?

# Finale


O my mustard-lipped Tytania,
Do you understand why our toes are growling like cornered rats?


Are you ready, O my magnetic controversy,
To kiss

    O!

      O!

        Hee-haw!

Kiss
Kiss,
One by one,
Upside down
In a nutshell,
The flashing apple,
Scars,
Cartilage and omnipotence
Of the singular,
New
Rising
Sun,

    Before

        the universe

            breaks

                up?

# Silenus

## A Pseudo-Mythological Extravaganza in Three Parts

The wind blows to the south,
and goes around to the north;
around and around goes the wind,
and on its circuits the wind returns.
—Eccles 1:6

83

Although a minor character in classical mythology, Silenus can be considered the archetype of universal wisdom. He is said to have been the tutor of Bacchus and king of the fabulous land where the young god was brought up. He was both a drunkard and a seer, renowned for his prophetic power and his ability to tell extraordinary tales. One day he was taken prisoner by some shepherds, who forced him to tell them stories that only the gods knew. King Midas, wanting to learn the secret of human life, ordered that Silenus should be admitted to his presence. Silenus revealed to him things no human being had ever known before. In this poem Silenus is a new post-urban prophet.

# Part 1
# Debut

Unformed,
Deformed,
O ruby nymphs,
Explain my complexity to these geometrical hordes,
Because if they can understand that north and south are only two
     of the seven streets of the sky—
As everything depends on the right perspective—
Perhaps they will also understand the balance of my intentions
     and the sting of my long tail.

Although I have been contemplating pure divinity for two stone
     of centuries,
I am still bewildered:
If I consider the absolute weight of illusions and the arrows of
     time,
I can inevitably conclude that they are less divine than your acne
     scars.

To you and no one else, my nymphs,
Who once told me you longed to kiss my soporific hair,
I, who was born when the Roman Empire could be crammed into
     a chamberpot,
Dedicate my topaz yawns,
My persistent effects.

In my grandfather's coffer I found a grotesque bone,
History's femur;
I bored three holes in it,
My new pipe was ready.

I decided to sneak out of prestige and sleep rough for once,
Sylvan comfort under a waving tin roof:
You should have seen me, well-combed and scented with chlorine
    and sulphur,
My tie attracting neutrons and dragonflies.

I made for the station at the bottom of Sunset Boulevard—
A hyperbolic name I can hardly account for,
Because it is a haunt of tipsy satyrs and hermaphrodites,
Or perhaps another philosophical subtlety.

I was dazzled by the mysticism of empty condom packets on onyx
    benches;
I chose a freight train pulling out unnoticed from a dead-end track,
Doomed wagons in the jingling moonlight,
Destination: Arctic Forest.

I jumped on and made a pillow of some waving flakes I saw in a
    corner,
Each bridge we flew across added a bar to the night overture;
I slept soundly until something familiar awakened me,
A stream of radioactive jam petting my feet.

*

Darling, my scarlet nymph,
Sometimes I wonder if you are happy when I show you my iron
    impertinence,
No one can interpret the alphabet of your panties.

Both minutes and millenniums are reflected in the polished
    globes of your breasts,
Nothing more than intestinal hieroglyphs,

Flimsy faith:
Cyclic meridians and parallels through my hallucinations like
    transgressive spasms,
Pensive smoke enriching my contemplative pause,
Gamma rays, a nocturne in my receptive ears.


From my throne on a rubbish crag,
Attached lavatory and potato patch,
I contemplate my idyllic island:
From gates of petrified sweat to the essence of typhoid fever,
My artery-kingdom.


I choose another bottle of top-class Bordeaux to celebrate the sac-
    rifice of a new day,
The conscience of a crazed huddle of muscles and tensions,
Poisonous embryos.


When I say good morning, I mean something quite improbable;
When I lift my cup and wait, there is a whole symphony between
    the moments:
A draught and I drink half of the world,
Political dystrophy, catechism and all.


I do not think a thousand good mornings will ever nourish the
    new-day mob;
From the apogee of my enterprise, I'll try offering free tickets for
    my ethical triumph.


*


. . . and good morning to you, my boy.

If only you had listened to me,

And you had gone to bed before draining the third bottle, instead
    of leaping from hole to hole dressed up as a peacock, sucking
    cigarette butts and licking chocolate wrappings,
You wouldn't be an asymmetrical frog now.

Will you ever understand that it is despicable to fish a hospital
    dump for second-hand organs?
Or pay a prostitute before telling her you are divinely impotent?

When will you understand that you are a god in disguise?

*Hillary, pillory, sock,*
*The head was on the block . . .*
                    Well,
When the sun burns over orange puddles and dazzling heaps of
    social litter,
I'll teach you to revolutionize levels and systems,
And suck the sinuous nectar of aeons.

Lesson 36—Revision:
In the intoxicated factory yard, the core of the universe,
Nothing can stop my rage:
I yell,
Wriggle,
Perjure,
Around the cultural bonfire.

Without ostentation,
You must pile, my boy,
All you think is righteous and functional,
And with no regret
Set fire to the plateaus with your fresh pair of purple eyes.

Before we discuss our mechanical meditations,
Let's sum up:
You can both grill the principles of gravity and rephrase the seven
    shades of light,
As long as you never profane my kegs of Arcadian ale.

# Part 2
# Scherzo

Have you bought what the voice in my dream told us to buy for
    our guest's meal?
                        Aha!
Frantic salad (all our savings!)
Three tubs of
Mountain prawn &
Indonesian wine,
A twenty-pound pearl-cake,
Rivers of
        tangerines
                and implacable dustbin berries.

I would also like to add a pinch of vehemence
To help his fever ferment.

How strange!
We didn't have the heart to squeeze anything from his pompous
    nose,
Out of our car-wreck lair,
Our knives sweating turpitude,
Glinting ambiguously.

"Fill our bags with iridium buttons!" we bawled.

*Oooh!* And
He fell into a steaming pool
                              Ha! Ha!
Laughing green and pink in the moonlight dripping from the
    roofs around the courtyard.


Were I a king, as you claim,
Do you think my hands would be melon rind,
My paunch a saucepan where the capital vices are boiled without
    a drop of holy water?
I only have a few coloured chalks,
A pouch bulging with tales.


Let your imagination crunch the main tendon of logic,
And let's close our deal:
A meal rich enough to feed a dozen gods in return for one of my
    heavenly yarns!


                              *

Once upon a time when the world was flat,[2]

---

2. This story told by Silenus is inspired by a twelfth-century legend
about the Italian wine Est! Est! Est! (Latin for "It is! It is! It is!"), pro-
duced at Montefiascone. It is said that a German bishop had to go to
Rome for the coronation of Henry V. He liked drinking very much, and
he knew that very good wines were produced in Italy. He decided to
send one of his servants ahead to identify every inn on the way to Rome
where good wine was served. When the servant encountered good wine,
he had to write the word "Est!" on the front door of the inn to inform his
master. At Montefiascone, some fifty miles north of Rome, the servant
found such a superb wine that he wrote "Est! Est! Est!" When the bishop
got there and read the words, he could not believe his eyes, and he drank
so much of that excellent wine that he died.

The sky a turquoise lid, the sea a silver plain,
Sir John Galore, renowned professor of theology, set off for a
    southern paradise,
Where the Tiber spread its wings over apple trees, grapes, and
    dead volcanoes,
In search of some relief from his rheumatic quips.

A sun-kissed hospital:
O short cut to seventh heaven and biblical reincarnation!

"My backside needs soft armchairs,
My liver an immunizing elixir:
I'll only die when I meet the god who invented wine."

How incongruous life is!
The god I met was no leaf-crowned Bacchus,
No hairy Priapus,
No sweaty Falstaff,
But a green-haired Circe:
Crossbow mouth,
King-size brassiere,
Fatal eyelashes.

Can an empire be crumbled by cherry lips and a glass of wine?

"O Señorita Francisca, having visited your palace amid olive
    groves at the chirping hour,
Shall I wish for more?

"Nothing to complain about, Señorita:
The pheasant you serve is Solomon's voice,
Your breasts need neither pepper nor spices.

"Hooray for your hors d'oeuvres,
For the hypnotizing serenade of your barrels,
When our souls caper about with your lullabies!"

But what became of Sir John Galore once he had drained all Fran-
    cisca's wine,
Two gold florins a demijohn?

In truth, my friends,
I've never been good at weaving epilogues,
I prefer playing pranks on pushers and pimps in Helicon Street,
Snaring rats while dreaming of my nymphs' underwear . . .

Floating in those flowery waves,
Drunk as a squid,
He dissolved like magnesia,
In the reiteration of a reed rustling
In the August
Breeze.

What moral can be drawn now I really don't know,
For a seer is unable to explain his visions—
Either a sixty-carat sapphire
Or a spoonful of
Arsenic.

# Part 3
## Oration

"What is happiness?" asked King Midas, lord of bridges,
Putting out his sumptuous cigar in a pilchard tin,
His crutches creaking in a puddle of paraffin,

Camphor gurgling in his throat:
The whole cosmos was vaporizing in that virgin yard.

Napping nexuses,
Proportion and value,
A fistful of sand tinkling in a rusty kneecap.

"O Silenus, old archetype,
Are my walnuts disturbing the night voyage of your thoughts?"

The wind brought the call of a cargo ship,
A bulldozer growling in a desolate building site.

Everyone knew that all the king's power was in a leather case un-
    der his nuts-and-bolts bed:
Blade and
Veneration;
Yet there was something no one could identify,
Workmen's clavicles dumped in a Byzantine refectory.

"Tell me—
        Tell me!
How old is the rainwater in my cupped hands?"

I remember now:
Mr. Herod lived next door,
Number 117,
At the head of the stairs, a small cave in the roof,
Door 8 or 7½.

After dark,
He would creep out of his chemistry den,

Walk away on a carpet of shade,
His grey raincoat heavy with ages of wind and sleet.

"I only love stray souls down London Bridge:
Women only hide razors under their skirts."

And always smiling piously,
To his meatballs he would add a few drops of strychnine.

If I am lucky enough and the wind is favourable,
It is easier for me to sit on a flagpole and spit at all those generals
     on parade in Parliament Circus
Than listen to a priest's homily and be sanctified.

Mankind belches and breaks wind without blushing,
But what a surprise!
The village fool thinks he has been eating caviare,
While his stomach is full of onions.

Philosophers and diviners have failed:
Their endeavours are drying out like socks in the backyard.

But will the poet-tribe ever fail?

At the bottom of the street, where a sibyl used to own a radio sta-
     tion in a basement,
A beggar is playing rummy by the light of a silver hydrant:
Our days are at stake,
There is no way of beating him,
No way.

Do you want to bet?

*Silenus*

*

When I was a child along the tinkling fence,
Although I was unable to save more than 5p a week,
I always had enough money to buy miraculous toys.

Once I bought a flying rug for a half-crown,
A gold padlock for a useless shilling:
They must still be in my cellar, 23 Helicon Street.

Why don't you squander your money—Father would say—on
    something cheaper and more essential?
The tables of financial martyrdom:
Have you learned to interpret them yet?

Warehouse 59, my official hideout,
*Boris Falieri Inc.* still visible on its door;
I laid out all my whims on a rotting shelf,
Telescope and mental cables;
Three small windows were enough for my appetite,
I could see the night tides and the infinite bay,
Steamers sailing for the Antilles,
All I had always dreamed of.

I spent hours watching a tugboat being sanctified,
A workman saw me—Poor little kid!
And he gave me a wooden mace to play with.

To get a groaning perspective on experience,
I perched on a high-tension pylon;
I recited the borders of all the city quarters,
And after a glance at the spires of the children's museum,
I took to turning about the backyard along with the ethical dust.

I am by no means different from that child,
When he saw his reflection in a basin of rainwater and promised
   he would never grow up.

*

The golden eagle lives on the cold plateaus,
Observes the migration of seasons,
No one around him;
There are only burrows and bazaars beyond the horizon,
The wind is a solemn harp.

I jump from roof to roof,
Where I can take a break under the palm tree of knowledge:
"No, thank you, I never eat fruit—only parsnips!"

As my final step,
Let me cram time and faith into an unbreakable jar,
And seal the lid forever and ever:
NOT TO BE OPENED TILL ETERNITY.

Now, if you will excuse me,
I must mix a cocktail of sparkling seconds,
For what I deserve most is a meaningless spree
And a comfortable hammock
Between Notre Dame
And the cliffs of purgatory.

# Epicurus

## Poetic Fragments

His only aspiration was to a felicity so high
that it seemed almost unrealizable on this earth.
—Joseph Conrad, *Nostromo*

# Preamble

It had been snowing all night,
The end of that cold, atypical November,
So many years ago that hardly anyone living those days is alive
    today,
When I saw his creeping shadow on the snow,
Silently creeping to my uncle's garage,
And in the light of a circular window sitting on a pile of tyres,
Taking shelter from the wind and hooking flakes.

All the remarkable events in my life happened after a snowfall.

My birthday was unknown,
I was found in a basket under a streetlamp early one morning,
On Saint Ralph's day, someone even swears—
That's why, perhaps, I love slum songs so much . . .

# Epicurus' Aphorisms

A perfect woman is a lobster stew,
Rare,
Priceless
Puzzlingly priceless,
Only served on Mount Everest
In oaken bowls.

*

Remorse
Is a moth in a box of silk hats,
But unfortunately evil
Is not a mustard stain on a napkin.

*

Human nature more or less boils down to this:
Men unzip their trousers,
Then perhaps fall in love;
Women think they are in love,
Then offer free flowers to strangers:
Both are wrong.

# Analysing Some Basic Principles
# of Middle-Class Neurosis

First of all, are *inconsistency* and *bourgeois* synonyms?
A jellyfish attitude would be excusable here,
For no one will ever relate them to a fourteenth-century mademoi-
    selle methodically sitting by the fireplace,
Embroidering,
Figurative excrescence of a castle on a hill overlooking the Loire.

If everything—
Although *everything* is such an impropriety of style,
Low-class generalization—
But if everything depended on the silk variety of her expectations,
Or fanciful panties at least,
Would you admit that she is a bourgeois icon despite the prototyp-
    ical furniture in her boudoir?

Papa has taken care of all the details,
And details are not elusive,
If you are halfway between Odysseus returning home from the
    Cyclops Club
And King Oedipus, who has just realized that he might have mar-
    ried the wrong woman.

Unpredictable rainy day in July,
An unconventional moment to buy a plane ticket to New York,
First-class flight,
Rose petals as a treat,
Unicorn milk for breakfast,
Geisha in the ladies' room.

Bon voyage!
Remember
      A postcard to Mama . . .

It sounds like an archetypal lullaby,
Or was it just a stale catchphrase hummed by an old tart while she
     was being raped in Jack the Ripper's convertible after an ice-
     cream orgy?

(Whenever I have to define a woman—
Negatively, of course,
Meticulously running the risk of being labelled as a misogynous
     camel,
Or worse than that, ostracized—
I am usually embarrassed:
Dictionaries are benevolent,
With inventories of terms ranging from the most classical twists,
Plebeian sophistication,
To those with a delicate shade of professional austerity;
But I always pick the one that has always reminded me of a picnic
     in the Victorian countryside,
Slices of strawberry toast,
Goldfinch eggs in ivory eggcups,
Traditional sherry,
Moderate bouquet.)

# A Trip to Hell

I'll lead you into the dungeon of human nature, where psychologi-
   cal villains are punished,
Among bottles of rancid wine and moth-eaten wigs,
Spirals of squeaking steps,
Down,
Down,
Down,
        D
            o
                w
                    n
Whispers,
Syncopated sighs,
Raucous alliterations . . .

In the light of a three-watt bulb I saw them,
Huddled together in a corner, hundreds of them,
Rats in a gas chamber.

Nailed to the central heating boiler,
Solitary, nodding his head,
One of my mother's most loyal friends,
Mr. Caruso, a nightclub doorman, swollen and grunting, a scalped
   swine.

I remember the day we found out he was going to run away with
   my fourteen-year-old sister:
While he was howling on a young cherry tree in blossom,
My father shot him in the back,
Singing Puccini in a compassionate voice.

The next morning my father told the police Mr. Caruso had left
    for the Andes,
Silk ties, cigars, and ten hip flasks in his trunk.


O! Glory! Glory!
Another bucket of dog's waste ascended to hell!
And we all went to bed imbued with religious benevolence.


In the darkest niche, where my uncle would store his barrels of
    smuggled brandy,
Chained to a rusty bicycle, a worn-out boot,
One of my beloved schoolmates—what was his name?—
Boys regarded him as Al Capone reincarnated,
Girls thought he was Odin's youngest son;
In contrast, I thought he was a gnat on my chicken sandwich.


O!
   O!
      O!
Maybe after a cocktail party or at my stylish bungalow on Green-
    wich hill, where I studied archaeology or renaissance acupunc-
    ture,
Social etiquette, tribal adaptation,
She slipped off her knickers as she nibbled her apple pie:
Wasn't that enough for my amour-propre?
     O!
   O!
O!


But . . .
      unfortunately,
It wasn't like breaking wind in a Victorian hall during a harp solo:

You open the window and everything is once again crystal and
    sparkling,
A basket of pansies and hummingbirds.

Hang him!

My erect penis, the most convenient gibbet,
As from the shining mast of a pirate ship.

I have always dreamed of becoming a captain like Francis Drake,
He once had his Italian chef thrown to his loyal barracudas when
    he found a mummified finger in his chowder.

Ha! Ha! Ha!
My hatred, as pure as a thorn in Snow White's navel,
A sacred arrow stuck in God's calf!

Come on, my boy—said my wise guide—let's walk on,
She was only a poor country slut,
And he, hyperbolically speaking,
Just a shovelful of
Low quality
Leprosy.

## Love Hypotheses

The maid was in keeping with the tallest fir tree in the mystical
    forest,
Her eyes the same colour as the jug of wine she brought us.

"I can give you everything you need," she said,
But what I actually needed, she was unable to give:

Let's ride together around snow-capped casks and impenetrable
    nightmares.

We were strolling through photographic alleys, side by side,
Palpable abstractions;
How many lovers have you had since last summer?
She smirked, circling the treetops with her long claw.

*

Saturday night out with my next girlfriend on the list,
A call at the nearby Pizza House,
Then something quite ordinary for a change.

I park somewhere inspiring and unpoetic,
She unzips my trousers and on she goes with accuracy,
Perhaps Cinderella was used to doing the same.

*

When you said you'd already had a dozen lovers,
I imagined a fashionable café and you talking about *Le Roman de la
    Rose* or Dante's *Vita Nova?*
O! Why are you anxious about your HIV test?

## One Night at the Suicide Hotel

Mr. Mayakovsky across the street,
A tall, black-haired artist,
Eyes of a Siberian wolf,
His atelier among the chimneys,
I usually met him on my way to school every morning;
The news reported that he had blown his brains out in front a ba-
    roque mirror, while drinking a glass of warm Merlot.

His neighbours had rarely seen him around,
A few friends and a French whore;
An empty envelope was found among his sketches,
His grief an untreatable blade.


*


At the old baker's shop, one morning last July,
Some people whispering bits of strange conversation,
Father Blackroot had died the night before at the age of ninety-
    nine,
Dreaming about an ebony tankard of stout.


*


The bounty hunter prepared his weapons with care,
Tins of Brazilian spam, peanuts, cans of perry in his sack,
Two black-and-white photographs:
*Fag Frank: $200,*
*Silver Condom: $400;*
Enough to spend a weekend on,
Far away from his Dead Sea depression.

He set off at dawn,
He waited eight hours in his pick-up truck after setting his trap,
An iron rod in the frosty morning.

When he returned at four o'clock the next day,
He had two dripping heads in his sack:
Not worth much, I know,
But he had never had such fun.


*


It was time for him to sacrifice his most vigorous hog,

He chose the sharpest knife from his kitchen drawer.

While the blood was spurting out into a sacramental dish:
What if it was a reincarnated sinner?

*

No moon in the sky,
A few scattered stars,
I walk silently,
Thinking of how my life could have been if I had met different
    people,
If you had met different people.

I close my eyes,
Breathe in deeply,
And jump in front of the roaring lights fast approaching in the
    distance.

*

We tiptoed to the door and peeped inside,
The old man was sitting at the kitchen table,
Stirring his cold milk in a trance,
Gaping at the ivory circles evoked by his spoon.

He did not understand why his mother had dropped him at school
    early that morning,
And now he was there, stirring his cold milk;
He remembered he did not want to go to school that morning,
He wanted to stay at home and play with his new Batman doll.

Someone had promised him happiness and fame,
It was a Creole palmist, when his father took him to the circus one
    summer night many years before,

Fame and happiness,
A long nail,
A vial of cyanide . . .

*Sleeping Beauty* isn't just a metaphor, is it?
Do you know what the prince said—
A peculiar fellow, not very keen on second-hand cars, washing
     machines, and cigarettes—
When he awakened his princess with a chaste kiss on her lips?

An improbable conclusion, underground and naive,
A bowl of muesli at midnight,
My favourite one.

That night I threw up all night,
And first thing in the morning,
I decided to hang myself in the shower,
As drunk as an overcooked lobster . . .

# Black Petrol

*Black Petrol*


In the name of
sideways repercussions
and gaseous trinity . . .
Amen!


Is that Mr. Rasputin?
I can preach another memorable sermon for you,
Certainly not the last of my audacity:


From now forth, until Lucifer plays a Liszt rhapsody on your ribs,
You'll dust your mirrors and candelabra yourself,
And you'll wax your planetary desk with your embroidered
    handkerchiefs;
The only thing I can still do for you is to mow your wife's lawn,
At my leisure, of course, after a ceremonial booze-up.


As for that weekly handful of quid, which only allowed me to be
    different from a Himalayan tramp—
Incidentally, why haven't you given me a rise since I polished the
    parquet in your velvety-walled privy fourteen years ago?—
Put it aside to buy a brand-new set of mechanical slaves!


I'll be seeing you at the next monetary eclipse,
Auf Wiedersehen!
I am going to reshape myself into a collective angel.


*


As always, the commuters' train called at Crude Oil Inn at 8:30,
She got on punctually and sat down opposite me, all bright with
    hypothetical diagrams;
All the time I dreamed of her long legs, as long as the Nile's waves,
Until I decided that she would become my next intransigent muse.


111

While she read her Monday paper, I wandered across her evasive
    dimensions,
Without leaving out the holiest recesses of her chemical structure,
    which I explored with minute interest;
By the time the train pulled in, I no longer remembered my name
    and address,
But I had learned the names of all her hypochondriac lovers.

I am sailing the South China Sea next summer, are you going to
    come with me?
A friend of mine is a sea wizard there, although he only owns a
    small fish shop in Melville Close;
When there is no drinkable water in July, he migrates to the bor-
    der towns, preaching the transition of winds;
He once sat up all night to watch a bunch of old sailors paint the
    keel of their yacht amaranth and black, black and amaranth:
Come with me, and we'll catch up with him before he reaches the
    Great Wall and the paddy fields beyond.

Lend me £50 and we'll manage to run off together one way or
    another,
I can afford a necklace of varnished vertebrae to persuade you:
My sweet, it will be a magnetic summer, believe me;
It is so easy to play faro dangerously on the deck of a piratical
    junk.

Take off your bra and put on your emphatic sombrero,
I'll pick you up two minutes before sunrise,
Electric water on your saturated skin.

*

I have just assembled a perfect prototype,

Either an infrasonic tricycle or a six-wheeled dragon:
A thousand piston rods, human wires and valves,
A philosophical shock to make its chassis invulnerable,
Even a fully furnished sidecar for you to spend a complete honey-
    moon in whenever the fancy takes you.

You can sit beside me and enjoy the motorway illusions,
Even though you never keep your promises.

We'll soon be ready to take over every imaginary curve,
Every somersault of events,
And start the countdown:

15,000,000
       9,000,000
          3,000,000

Maybe 1,000,000 is a very promising number,
Not a penny less!
But you prefer dollars, do you?

Please don't think I'm going to have a week off because I want to
    study a prodigious aquarium somewhere on the east coast,
I never keep my promises either, but none of my lies has ever been
    wasted;
So
Let us eliminate
Every trace of perturbation from our redemptive friendship.

I don't know what you feel when you buy a pair of Ferragamo
    trainers,
I can only give you a fistful of epigrams.

You'd better highlight my inscrutable principles on your map,
Before we step into a new intangible order:

Nitroglycerine rolls,
Enough fuse to enclose Texas twice,
Petrol bombs in case we need an eccentric touch . . .

Could I borrow your lipstick to finalize my list?

*

"Remember," said the Judge, "not only your spirit but also your
    flesh has been infested:
We'll heal you for good, my lad, better than a troop of call girls."

I laughed while they took me away,
They were only maggots in uniform;
When they locked the door of my cell, I thought of you strolling
    on a pier of a Saturday evening, smiling;
You were quite right,
Only the sea can purify our innermost thoughts,
And this is a perfect day to fade away.

What do you think I thought
When I saw you walk barefoot on the coral pebbles into the cool
    sea foam?

Come on, let's meet up over there,
The blue bungalow overlooking the spiral mist.

What can you see from here, my sweet, the top of our century?
I'll show you the map of common mediocrity,
From the intolerance of a Hollywood ham on your right

*Black Petrol*

To the intestinal entropy of a pop band on your left,
But first of all, come closer and tell me:
Did you really add a pinch of supermodel's marrow to your stew?

*

My skin is a spotlessly clean looking glass,
Immutable, unflinching,
My hair quivering in the elastic wind:

"May I stay a little longer tonight,
And watch you doing the ironing,
Talking about an unusual holiday in Barcelona?"

You have always admired my commas and question marks,
The crisp sense of my breath,
Living anaesthetic.

You mingled with a crowd of inexplicable faces,
You neither stirred nor said anything,
But you loved me—of course you did!—for a few seconds,
Wondering about the value of your fingertips and the injurious
    gold of my bones.

*

All right, ladies and gentlemen,
Tonight I'll divine your future in a bowl of black petrol,
So that all of you can be confident of betting on a top-class dog,
Or invest £500,000 without anxiety:
You are more likely to come across a middle-aged trollop who
    leaps from one bed to another in her cosmic attempts to ma-
    terialize a Tibetan theorem,
Than have a chat with an honest councillor.

115

I gnaw,
Scratch,
And spit:

In the name of my snare drum,
Let all those gentlewomen in their well-earned mink coats
Come to me, O herds of insolent cattle!
Their husbands, plastic moguls on the brink of suicide,
Their ruby-ribboned pussycats,
Their nausea.

I can explain to all of you why I love Croesus and his three daugh-
    ters so much,
Perhaps you will all understand that a thoroughbred is not so dif-
    ferent from a mongrel,
When your stomach is as empty as a hydrogen atom.

My lethal enemy was sitting in the middle of an unreachable
    circle,
Amid elegant sophisms printed on sepia postcards,
A compass pointing to the cerebral north on a page,
His words sharper than a cheese knife.

"My mission in life is to preserve the impulses of humanity,
But what is here concocted is only sparrow's droppings;
And you, why are you playing with unwieldy mechanisms?"

I once read about a civilized tribe who sold embalmed heads as
    souvenirs
To add a classy touch to a mantelpiece in Louis XVI style:
Is it a sophisticated whim to exhibit the geniuses of our times in a
    country tearoom?

# Epilogue

I don't half understand ye: what's in the wind?
—Herman Melville, *Moby-Dick*


Content with my psychotic prospect,
I can now relax on my sofa sipping some regimental bliss,
My long-legged muse in a Machiavellian G-string at my side, pe-
    rusing a financial pull-out:
Are you ready to mock the Chancellor of the Exchequer?
If only I didn't need your veneration so much,
I would auction it off to recoup some of my former days.


If you feel like it, stand up and leave in silence,
But please, don't tell me that your lost boyfriend has finally re-
    turned from Baghdad with a forty-carat stone for your wed-
    ding ring:
You bore me to death!


O my immune assistant, in the meantime,
Since I have never belonged to a single entity,
Keep on decorating my feet to expiate your carnal chores:


My finale will be an ambulance
At breakneck speed
Into the night.

# Light-Heartedly

## Scattered Stanzas

# Modest Overture
## (After Vladimir Mayakovsky)

And then you came like a pack of rabid dogs at dawn,
Sudden,
Ravenous,
Disruptive,
A glass splinter in my right eye,
A cursed arrow in my neck.

You wanted to eat my testicles like grapes,
But nonetheless I welcomed you,
Although I was a cautious conformist,
Double-breasted suit, straw heart,
And very little else.

So you came and said, "Let's play!"
But you did not wait and you took me by the hand,
And off you pulled me to the swings behind the school,
A sacrilegious session on a misty morning:

*Jack be cunning,*
*Jack be smart,*
*Jack don't listen*
*To that tart!*

Come on, let's kick those children off their seats
And take over the playground!

But, O my Laura, O bright star!
Peeing in the sandpit can hardly be glossed as an act of political
    rebellion.

# My Imaginary Self

The alarm clock mocks me unsympathetically,
I get up and shuffle to the kitchen and drink some oily stuff from a
　　jug,
Imitating another shantytown poet who did the same.

I don't need to shave,
I don't need to change my clothes,
I don't need a clean shirt or to comb my hair,
Just a knotted rope, an inflatable whore chained to my bedpost,
And one after another, an endless sequence of attempts,
And then a long unconscious spell.

Now you, common-sense people,
You who shout at me, "Cheap poseur!"
You, damned hypocrites!
It is just the same with all of you:
The truth is nothing I have really belongs to me,
And nothing you have really belongs to you.

And you, Mother, why don't you stick a straw into my skull and
　　suck my brain?
Is there anything else beyond a Virgin Mary doll?
Can she cure my heartburn once and for all?

It is because of the ring you dropped into my cereal bowl, isn't it?
Did I really swallow it this morning at breakfast?

Doctor, what's wrong with me?

Here is your prescription, boy:

*Incoherent principles twice a day,*
*Watermelon breasts and buttocks,*
*Roadrunner legs;*
*And if you feel you can't go to the loo carelessly,*
*A pinch of capricious tongue in your ear.*

## So to Speak

And then—I was saying—you came and said,
"I am a mathematician and nothing more."

But your leopard legs gave you away:
"I dance around, along with the Brazilian breeze."

The ripples of your impertinent skirt as you strut away,
Your flying fingers when you light a cigarette—
You baffle me!
You can be either,
You can be both,
Or a thousand other incarnations,
And although I may sound quite conventional:
A rag bonfire nymph,
An underground station witch,
A junkie lily of the vale,
Savage nitrogen.

There is no way I can stop comparing you,
Especially when you put on your black leather skirt,
And I watch you walk upstairs triumphantly—
Are you wearing any underwear?

Please don't move,

Just stay there, in front of the mirror and take a snapshot,
Black panties and a pink ribbon,
A cellophane veil wrapping up your bouncing breasts,
King-size trout on sale on a market table.

Don't you think there's something unconventional about talking
     on the phone while you are shaving your legs,
Or mixing a piña colada at five o'clock?
And why do you think I should be indifferent when you step into
     your bath like a backstreet Messalina?

Let's hijack a plane to Costa Rica, Guatemala, or wherever the sun
     grills you like chicken wings and scorpions crawl into your bed
     uninvited,
Nothing to live on but margarita, lambada, and diamonds,
Because you are unprejudiced and unorthodox—
Am I not?

"What if I got married in a couple of months?
Yes, anywhere, anyhow . . .
The first man who tells me I'm a princess even if he thinks I'm a
     wayward slut;
After all, marriage is only a bourgeois simplification,
And love another lyrical illusion.

"Do you know what I'm going to do tonight?
Details should never be disregarded,
So guess, mon petit chou!"

Now while you are pottering about the kitchen,
Still in your pink dressing gown, although it is nearly five o'clock
     in the afternoon,

Pink woollen socks and pink fluffy slippers,
Do you mind answering my question honestly?

Why do you like the crack of the word *slut* so much?
And if I repeated it over and over again,
A cultivated distortion of the far more prosaic *darling*,
It would not be an annoying lack of taste,
Because even the moment you hike up your skirt and show me a
    swollen spot on your shaven groin can be paraphrased into a
    metaphysical confirmation of the absurdity of the *What's-in-a-
    name* Quartet,
Which is so poetically close to a pinch of John Donne's puns.

We drank a lot and laughed until midnight,
Sea food and sparkling wine,
Could we have some more ice, please?

But why was it necessary for you to phone your low-class prince?

Your inability to attach any significance to these prophetic signs is
    a disturbing incongruity:
                A second-hand BMW convertible,
                An unsolvable chemistry test,
                A lecture on the origin of the universe,
                Some surrealist graffiti on your car's boot . . .

Since nature is not such an old-fashioned concept,
Please stop sighing a second and consider:
Can you really understand the difference between
                An apostrophe
                    and
                A comma?

# Short Conversation about Men, Women, and Other Rubbish

To start with, the following axiom would be effective:
"When a woman stops regarding her man as a miracle,
Everything is over."

Is it?

Granted, nobody can be Prince Charming 24/7,
But most men are dull and unsubtle from the start;
What if you think you are a unique genius?
Who cares!
There will always be a brass-faced bitch out there eager to fart on
    your genius face—
Light-heartedly!

In short, everything depends on a pair of high heels,
Or an appropriate choice of stockings,
The first thing you notice when you catch the icebreaking
    glimpse,
Even though nothing serious is going on later;
A woman can be everything—
Milk and honey,
A cyanide pill,
But especially—and brutally—legs and buttocks,
And her choice of stockings can make the difference;
But, trust me, it's rock-hard to go any deeper:
Please, darling,
Try your hand at something
More florid and meaningful than
*You snore like a wild boar!*

# (Un)Plausible Epilogues

The first attempt at an epilogue is usually squalid and banal,
Only inspired by the $10,000,000 question:
"What the hell does a woman want?"

If I bought a plane ticket for Acapulco and a seven-star hotel suite,
I would be extremely predictable,
But I think *that* is the thing you really want.

And now, please give me a gun;
A polished revolver with one immaculate bullet in the cylinder,
Yes! Just one pious bullet!
Am I asking for too much?

Will you get annoyed if I blow my brains out here,
Just here, in your Chippendale sitting room?
The only inconvenience, I know,
A gallon of freshly spilled blood,
And sorry, I won't be able to clean up the whole mess;
No legal drawbacks, though—
I promise you!

Perhaps a blade would be a more decorous choice,
A razor blade, shining and dignifying,
Far more exciting to handle than your clitoris;
How long would it take?
Ten minutes?
Twenty?
Half an hour?
I can sit still in a hot bath and watch my blood oozing out,
And dream . . .

Dream of what we would have been if—
If only I had not been such a ruthless bastard—
If only I had been born elsewhere . . .
IF . . .

# Artemis

## A Sequence

She seem'd, at once, some penanced lady elf,
Some demon's mistress, or the demon's self.
—John Keats, *Lamia*

# Meeting Artemis

She walked across the mystical foyer,
A forest of legs, bracelets, beads, and wrought-iron lamps,
Smoke and fractal fragrances, between the acts,
*Othello* premiere on a Sunday night,
In her blood-red minidress and high heels,
Strutting into the theatre bar like a priestess,
Perhaps a sacred lancet, gold-eyed and sapphire-haired,
Tattooed antelope, while I was draining my late-night drink:
She sat down by me and crossed her legs and asked,
"Am I the first woman you've fallen in love with?"

# Artemis at the Gym

Olympus is not a mountain, but a princely mansion,
A gymnasium for nymphs, gods, dukes, and queens,
In the leafy neighbourhood of a coastal city.

"This is a golden ticket for a trial class,
Please visit us at your convenience."

And when I turned up after my lunch break,
She welcomed me, brass tights and brassiere,
A whip and daggers hanging from her belt,
A chain collar around her neck and a nail in her navel.

"Come with me, there's a secret room down the corridor,
And if you're meek enough, I'll show you what I can do
With my whip and daggers, boots and chains,
And I'll let you worship my war tattoo upon my foot,
Which I but reveal to those who are about to die!"

# Showtime at the Arcade

Instead of bushes, meadows, twittering silence,
Only tall shelves full of gloves, T-shirts, socks, and compasses;
Her hair floating in the static breeze,
In latex leotard, Artemis was riding a symbolic bike,
While a suntanned Adonis was handing out flyers to passers-by:

OLYMPUS GYMNASIUM
WOULD YOU LIKE TO BECOME A GOD?
OPEN 24 HOURS
FROM NOW TILL THE END OF THE WORLD:
JOIN US!

From behind a plastic olive tree,
A new Tiresias was watching her;
He thought she was naked although she was not,
For he could feel every electric impulse crossing her muscles
And read her innermost doubts and anxieties.

"O! I do not care much about *if* or *when* or *why*,
About rules, logic, what is right, what is wrong,
Because there is nothing beyond your lashes now,
Your lips moving, your legs, belly, breasts, neck,
Your perspiration, as sharp as a gladius, uncompromised,
Spring splinters, a tinkling rill down your back, untainted rift.

"Can you feel my hands tearing your soul to shreds,
Slowly, layer by layer, like a worn-out nightdress,
To seize the paleness of your spiritual intimacy?
As long as they last, these moments are immaculate,
Meaningful, gleaming, and forever good."

# Dating Artemis

When he first saw her, he thought she was a Hollywood angel
Fallen all of a sudden from the clouds into his bed
While speeding across the sky in her white Rolls Royce
Because of a fierce paradisal storm.

Although her eyes were mountain ponds, unfathomable,
Her soul impalpable crystal, clear, transparent,
Hoarfrost on a balustrade, on the doorsteps at dawn—
She was not the woman he thought she was.

She was a snow leopard on the prowl,
Merciless, implacable, voracious,
A hunting knife, a howling night:
Her lips like fangs could rip his chest apart
And pick his heart out and throw it away,
Like a mutilated toy, a rotten apple.

Beware! Dating Artemis is a fatal act,
Challenging Achilles to a duel at sunrise in Hyde Park.

# Artemis on the Beach

Artemis does not spend her summers in the woods,
Hunting hares and wrestling with satyrs and wild pigs,
Oh no! She is quite an eccentric goddess,
And lies on the beach in her multicoloured bikinis,
Which have far deeper meanings than a Rimbaud sonnet:

In white, she is an ivory sword on a windowsill,
Unreachable idol on a chair of ice;

In yellow, a sunflower field, Van Gogh's vision;
In pink, a rose garden on fire in early June,
Lolita on her first day at high school;
In green, an emerald mantis, sugary poison on her lips,
Blowing ripples in a stiff pond;
In blue, Venus stepping out of a silken sphere;
In black, a panther roaring in a moonless close,
Dark dreams, unspoken secrets, overwhelming pangs;
In red, a tropical flood, eruption,
Nothing else than Satan's fiery fangs,
Forever burning bright in my bed all night . . .

# The Origin of Everything

## Or

## The Creation According to Moi-Même

## A Farcical Mystery

I am greatly indebted to Mr. Vladimir Mayakovsky, who visited the heavenly spheres in 1916 or 1917. However, I would like to point out that Mr. Mayakovsky's ascension took place millions of years after the Creation, while I was there just at the very moment everything began.

# 1

# (Inception)

When God created eternity in his poorly lit junkyard,
I was there,
Hidden behind the wreck of his old Porsche 356.

"Put on your new silk shirt!" Mother had said;
And she was right:
I honoured some torn tyres on the ground and vintage oil cans on
    display on a shelf.

No one can say what God looks like:
Perhaps a hermit on Mount Kilimanjaro,
A Mali shaman, Buddha's alter ego, or Gandhi's elder brother,
But I was hardly prepared to meet a scrap-metal scavenger.

What shall I call him?

*My liege,*
*Mr. Everlasting,*
Or simply
*Mr. Jack-of-all-trades?*

I wondered how long he had been sitting there,
In the glowing light of his Romeo y Julieta,
Mulling and musing, unable to make up his mind,
Maybe about two unstable syllogistic systems,
Or more pragmatically, whether to choose a stainless washer or a
    rusty camshaft,
"Oh, shit!" I heard him mumble. "If only I had created whisky, it
    could have helped me out!"

He stood up and scratched his bottom at last,
And after glancing around, he unbuttoned his breeches.

If he wished to rehearse Noah's flood,
Or it was due to that cold primaeval nothingness,
It's up to the reader to decide,
But Jesus!—and take my word for it—
The water his omnipotent bladder spurted out was nothing like
    Alice's tears:
Who would like to swim in that nauseous pool and be christened
    again?

Up I climbed a breakdown truck to watch the miracle of miracles
    take place,
Safe and dry and undisturbed.

Had the pope and all his cardinals been invited,
They would have revised all their sermons:
All in all, calculating the diameter of eternity,
Organizing neutrons and seconds in overlapping folders,
And conjuring up trillions of orbits in silence
Was just as easy as making an omelette—
Or even easier.

# 2
## (And Adam was All Alone, and So . . .)

There is a quiet nook at the bottom of God's junkyard,
A restricted universe for members only,
Usually frequented by Saint Augustine and his gang,
Three benches and a free fountain of illegal gin;
You can relax there for a dozen centuries,

And to your heart's content meditate upon the shape of human
    iniquity,
For it is always a quarter to five there.

Once I saw God himself taking a nap in his deckchair,
Exhausted with the ineffable efforts of his inventiveness,
In the shade of his woollen underpants hung out to dry.

"The chance of a lifetime!" I thought;
And avoiding the mousetraps laid in the grass,
I tiptoed to his garage and took a quick look at all his papers;
Pieces of chalk everywhere,
Tidiness was not God's main asset:
How had he managed to devise the depths of absolute zero with-
    out any noticeable glitch?

Some sketches were ingenious, I must concede,
But most of them utterly unfeasible:
A lawyer incapable of deceit,
A politician who loathed profit—
Just to mention a few examples.

Furtively I opened a small dog-eared journal on a stool:

*TUESDAY:*
*3:45 p.m. – Touch up the spring equinox*
*4:30 p.m. – Woman*
*5:00 p.m. – Man*

Who taught me that Adam had been created before Eve?
Where is the blueprint for the *woman* prototype?
Come on, let me take a sneak preview.

I examined everything with care,
My goodness! God must be joking!
This brainless goat wouldn't be good for a one-night stand!
What if I amended a few details?

God was a creative author, but an inaccurate editor;
Interpretation is an angelic power only bestowed on predestined
    souls.

I reduced the impedance of her brain circuits,
The convergence of her diverging nipples;
I increased the consistency of her night wishes;
Here and there I removed chunks of adipose tissue,
Trimmed wisps of unruly hair where inappropriate,
And added some foam rubber where necessary;
Although I tried to work as accurately as possible,
I might have made one mistake or two.

I went away whistling, proud of my inspiration:
Someone will certainly thank me one day;
I was now ready to try my hand at the eleventh wonder of the
    cosmos.

# 3

## (A Political Approach)

They were all sitting in silence around a boiling kettle on a stove,
The holy Maker in a woollen waistcoat and a score of his sidekicks;
Had someone told me, I wouldn't have believed them:
Gabriel, all muscles and perspiration, on the right,
A new waterfront hero,
And Lucifer—I bet it was him!—

A dishevelled drifter in a snakeskin jacket on the left,
Some more hard-boiled rogues all around them,
All of them suffering from scabies and pubic lice.

A vital item was on the agenda:
*Systems of government or, in other words,*
*The power of gold!*

"Eureka!" Gabriel said;
All the others looked up at him, yawning,
They had been racking their brains for over a thousand years but
    to no avail;
Without a cigar, a cup of coffee, or an ounce of nose stuff,
It is no laughing matter, believe me!

"Let's give the human race a first-rate commander,
His uniform glittering with dazzling dreams,
His nights boiling with political frenzy:
The welfare of those who worship him above all other things;
Everyone will work and produce,
Everyone will have sugared water,
Potatoes and sausages every day at lunch,
No one will ever complain."

"I propose," yelled someone else in shaking dreadlocks, "a bunch
    of crowned heads who attend charity balls every week,
And sail the skies in their winged yachts,
While monetary preachers plan years of peace and happiness:
Can you imagine a better illusion?"

"Enough!" And Lucifer rose from his seat,
Glowing like a freshly coined Napoleon:

"Yes, people need illusions more than anything else,
But everyone must feel impenetrably inspired,
And sleep well at night, confident and rewarded:
Why don't we create the *polling day*?"

An ice-cream kiosk in the middle of the Sahara wouldn't have
    been more welcome:
Everybody cheered,
God kicked the kettle and swore three times,
And they didn't draw lots this time.

I too had an interesting motion, but I didn't step forward,
I stole away unnoticed,
Trying to recall a political formula I had read in an old philosophy
    book.

# 4

## (Let's Go A-Scavenging!)

Whether it was the second or the third day of the Creation I was
    unable to tell,
One day could even last two million years,
Time was still a fluctuating concept.

As I didn't know what to do,
And I had still a great deal to analyse,
I ventured through a back gate,
Hoping to see the merry-go-round of proteins.

I walked down a potholed pathway;
Beyond a beta-ray fence the newborn universe bent to the right,
It was impossible to determine its true capacity.

Do you really think God was perfect?

I discovered the place where he had dumped his vain attempts,
At least twenty per cent of the whole inventory:
If I'd had enough inspiration,
I could have created a new universe by assembling that discarded
    junk.

There was, for instance, life-size samples of bankers;
At first sight they seemed all right,
But on closer examination I found out what was wrong:
Instead of grabbing, they were fond of giving!

On a heap of negatively charged protons,
I saw a booklet in vermilion ink:
A GUIDEBOOK TO PERFECT JUSTICE.

I was shocked, disconcerted;
One of my best friends is a High Court judge,
Another a middle-aged barrister,
We usually go pubbing together on Friday nights:
Is it possible they don't even know what justice really is?

I cleaned the booklet and shoved it into my pocket;
I wanted to show it to Gabriel and throw light on this case:
What slimy incongruity do we talk about in our law courts?

# 5

# (A Very Peculiar Virus)

"What's the matter with you, dear Satan?"
He was throwing Coca-Cola bottle caps into a pool of boiling oil,

He had even forgotten to put on his snakeskin jacket,
And there, on his right foot, you could see a mermaid tattoo still
    unfinished.

"God said my rank is at risk,
I am below heavenly standards;
I've been trying to work out a crafty scheme to impress him,
But I have failed."

"There is a way," I said,
"For I have a few nefarious tips that can match your greasy locks;
Just give me one of your rubber rings in return."

Satan stretched his majestic biceps,
"Wow!"
More similar to a street brawler than the King of Reptiles,
"Deal!"

"You need something worse than practical emotions,
Worse than investments and bank accounts,
Even worse than a ruthless oil company,
Something that might shock the centuries like cholera:
My friend, you need the recipe for
*Inspirational poetry!*"

# 6

# (Money & Fame)

"What's the difference between money and fame?" Satan asked;
God yawned and said, . . .
. . . . . . . . . . . . . . . . . . . . . . .
          *(Here the manuscript ends)*

# Irmegard

## Fragment of a Baroque-Punk Drama

In imitation of a poem by Stéphane Mallarmé

149

In his tragedy *Adelchi* (1822), the Italian author Alessandro Manzoni (1785–1873) called King Desiderius' daughter *Ermengarda*. In my opinion, the name *Ermengarda* has a sort of Gothic dignity, majesty, and haughtiness which *Desiderata*, the historical name of King Desiderius' daughter, does not convey. The name can be variously translated and spelled in English; I have chosen *Irmegard* as my favourite variant. For political reasons, Irmegard was forced to marry Charlemagne, but she was repudiated after a few months. This poem presents Irmegard's passionate rebellion against her arranged marriage, which makes her the first feminist rebel.

# Chorus

O sister!
Bosky promontories,
Sea-foam masked,
Necklace of sighs,
Let us have the power of salt,
Power of serpents in the wilderness,
To oppose
The meaningless,
Bronze-muscled
Moon.

Whose body is this?
Shining by torchlight,
Tyrant,
In the folds of my bed,
Both presage and sword,
Humiliating the efflux,
Sinless heart,
Like tentacular water?

# Irmegard and Mrs. Rosebush
# A Scene

Irmegard

    The corridors are swollen with purple vapour,
    Purple ellipses over pulsations and shapes,
    Where windows glitter, silence, memories,
    And artificial waves in moth whispers,
    And gardens below and flashes of neon agonies.
    Melodious, a lily of metallic ice.

I was floating in the smoke of brown roots,
Amongst wires and flying ravines, bride or bog siren,
Indifferent to the devotion of a mosquito tribe.
My mouth preserved reflections in a bottle;
Unconquered ivory, my legs bloomed in a field of rags;
My buttocks were dunes, my scales paraffin pearls,
Which some unguent had made ambivalent, almost haloes.
I wish I had stropped my razor in due course,
Although the grass was not yet submissive to it:
Yet what my mirror reflected was but a twisted riddle
Which I could no longer bear—no longer . . .
The breeze was blind; the lanterns were blind,
Upon my canopy only greedy lice contemplated my fleshless
    ribs:
What shall I offer to the ravens in my bed of rays?

Mrs. Rosebush

O! Your vestal seclusion, emerald
On the insensitive wings of a sooty bat:
You are the dream of draymen and slum dukes.
Believe me, when wrapped in their heretical mantles
The night patrol play dice and drink ammonia,
Like hermits stirring nebulae in a cauldron of sludge,
You are their inviolable goddess.
Your legs sustain the apse of coherence and crosses,
Your breasts like neurotic lutes make a sweeter melody than a
    poison sonata;
Your tresses on a sinister pillow, languidly indifferent,
Accepts the veil of glaciers into your young foliage.

Irmegard

I am sad and therefore motionless,

Motionless angel on this straw rug.
You can certainly tell me why
I ought to give away the whiteness of my mornings,
And die, perhaps shining with euphoric lightning,
But in a shroud of deformed slush.


MRS. ROSEBUSH

I, who have known you since your father's ferrets were fond of
    milk and cherries,
And have always offered aromatic morphine to your modesty,
I can no longer protect you from the horror of languid tongues.
How often have I hidden your beech breasts from the cries of
    crows in the woods and wolves on the hills?


IRMEGARD

I hoped nothing would rend your iron veil,
Would break your iron wire encircling my knickers.
Do you remember when I sat by the crossroads braziers,
Contemplating eddies of ashy days and my frozen gold?
O! I used to dream of lips like breeze, petals on my pillow,
And you promised words like beads for my white feet,
All around, strewn on the musical stream of my stockings,
All around, endlessly in the twinkle of minutes.


MRS. ROSEBUSH

Did I?—I only remember your locks dancing like sea worms,
Circular amoebas reflecting the symmetry of your skin,
Reflected amongst lamps of amazing mud:
The petals of your paleness were only false abstractions.
You are not doomed—trust me—to dissolution,
But you will reign over a waterfront paradise,
Forever draped in strips of eternity, scabbards, and syringes.

IRMEGARD

    Who is happier than a corpse swollen with acid wine?

    I am a signboard struck by an invisible bell-ringer.

    Please do not sit in your armchair, grotesque, as on an electric
        throne,

    Principles and proposals at your command,

    In your jewelled crypt, in the tremolo of your starry organs,

    The sonorous fluency of your juice—


MRS. ROSEBUSH

    What strange flames are shaking your brain?

    You think I am a sacred tiger, a twisting scimitar;

    No! I cannot stop the black star from swallowing the sun,

    And neither the water you stir with your morning hand,

    Nor any other prayer can ever soothe your howls!


IRMEGARD

    You have never loved me, then. Have you?


MRS. ROSEBUSH

    It is late, and I have other cases to attend to;

    Other bottles of fleeting alcohol and pickled nails.

    And you, poor embryo, you are still unthinkable,

    As if you had been sleeping for a thousand cycles,

    Where the wind mistook sawdust for gold . . .


# Litanies


O Lord, music in a diamond ladle.


It is time to celebrate our cuts and peroxide:
Have mercy on our black anguish!

We have seen beggar-women attired in meteors:
Have mercy on our black anguish!

Silk and lace tremble like molten drums:
Have mercy on our black anguish!

O Lord, scimitar and arboreal wisdom!

The rings of our chains are modesty and obedience:
Have mercy on our black anguish!

Modesty is a prostitute on a rocking horse:
Have mercy on our black anguish!

Obedience is a rat growing fat in our granary:
Have mercy on our black anguish!

O Holofernes, your head is shining like a ripe apple.

# Irmegard and a Fortune-Teller
## A Scene

IRMEGARD (*to herself*)
 Those neon nymphs, wriggling shapes on my crooked curtains,
 Segments and curves by the light of spicy froth,
 What treasures are they expecting to revel in?
 And when they show their fangs and tails on a flashing stage,
 A pulsing pole between the sky and the quicksand pool,
 Are they as holy and happy as I used to be?

(*Enter a Fortune-Teller carrying a small shoulder bag full of marbles. He
walks to a window, stops, takes some marbles out of his bag, throws them*

*in the air, and starts spinning them with his right hand as if they were
planets. When he sees Irmegard, he is surprised and tries to hurry away.)*

Wait! Don't be afraid of my scars.
Am I an immoral leper to run away from?

FORTUNE-TELLER

O! I pity your ripped stockings, your dripping heart,
The lake sand baking in your navel,
But I am not worthy to talk to you,
And purify the pimples on your neck.

IRMEGARD

I ought to love, O my comfort, the radiance of morning water,
But I hate it and love the bats hanging from my ceiling,
For a purulent mouth has tried to kiss me.

FORTUNE-TELLER

Look! I am old, a snake-haired vagrant,
Unable to prophesy immortality or melodious darkness;
I can only sell my delirium at street corners,
When these marbles, yellow
With monotonous virility, wallow
In pools of artificial harmonies.

IRMEGARD

Perhaps you are human, and your breath is human,
But the rain that makes your hair whisper
Is immortal, and I need its secrets as well as yours . . .

. . . . . . . . . . . . . . . . . . . . . . . . . . . . . . . . . . . . . . . . . . . .
. . . . . . . . . . . . . . . . . . . . . . . . . . . . . . . . . . . . . . . . . . . .
. . . . . . . . . . . . . . . . . . . . . . . . . . . . . . . . . . . . . . . . . . . .

Patrick Gasperini was born in Sidmouth, UK. He lives on the Continent now, where he works as an English teacher. He is the editor of *Locust Magazine* (www.locustmagazine.com), an online magazine of alternative art and literature.

www.facebook.com/PatrickGasperini1
www.facebook.com/locustmagazine

www.ingramcontent.com/pod-product-compliance
Lightning Source LLC
Chambersburg PA
CBHW021401150726
47989CB00005B/2340